Say & Glue for Language & Listening Fun Sheets

Written by Alyson D. Price, M.S.P., CCC-SLP
Edited by Amy Parks and Thomas Webber
Illustrated by Marty Schwartz

www.superduperinc.com
1-800-277-8737

ISBN 978-1-58650-364-2

Dedication

This book is dedicated to all of the family and friends that have cheered for and enthusiastically supported *Say and Glue*®, as well as encouraged the efforts of *Say and Glue*® *for Language and Listening Fun Sheets*!

To my parents, thanks for your overwhelming support, enthusiasm, and encouragement for both of these books. It means so much that you take great pride in all that I do.

To Jane, my number one cheerleader and promoter. What a great friend you are! Thanks so much for all that you do. Your friendship and enthusiastic support means the world to me.

Finally, to Jeff, Brittany, and Austin. Thanks for all of your support and enthusiasm for both of these books. I feel truly blessed to have such a great family. You guys are the best!

Introduction

After developing *Say & Glue*®, I realized the potential for a similar book geared more toward language-based therapy. This book targets children who have difficulty with various areas of language and language comprehension. It includes sections for categories, functions of objects, auditory processing (following directions and semantic recall), and basic concepts. Below is a list of ways to use the different activities in this book.

Categories

This section provides activities for children who have difficulty with categories. First, the child colors and cuts out the small pictures on the page. Then, the therapist/teacher reads each direction from the activity page to prompt the child where to glue each picture. For example, on the *Grocery Store* pages (pp. 2-3), the therapist/teacher reads the first direction, which prompts the child to find a fruit and glue it with the other fruits.

The thearapist/teacher may increase the level of difficulty by asking the child to choose a picture and tell the category of the item before gluing it with the items in that same category. For homework, the child takes home the finished page to practice naming all of the categories.

Functions

This section includes activities for children who have difficulty with naming the functions of objects. The child colors and cuts out the small pictures on the page. Then, the therapist/teacher reads each direction from the activity page to prompt the child where to glue each picture. For example, on the *Tool Shed* pages (pp. 12-13), the therapist/teacher reads the first direction which prompts the child to find something you use to cut wood and glue it on the page.

The therapist/teacher may increase the level of difficulty by asking the child to choose a picture and tell the function of it before gluing it on the page. For homework, the child takes home the finished page to practice telling the functions of each item.

Auditory Processing - Following Directions

This section offers activities for children who have difficulty following directions. It is broken into two parts, complex directions and conditional directions. The child colors and cuts out the small pictures on the page. Then, the therapist/teacher reads each direction from the activity page to prompt the child where to glue each picture.

In the complex directions section, the child listens carefully to a two-step direction before gluing the pictures on the page. For example, on the *Classroom* pages (pp. 30-31), the therapist/teacher reads the first direction which prompts the child to find the book and the apple. Then, he/she glues the book on the floor and the apple on the teacher's desk.

In the conditional directions section, the child listens carefully to the instruction, decides which one is correct, and glues the picture based on what was said in the directions. For example, on the *Playground* pages (pp. 62-63), the therapist/teacher reads the first direction which prompts the child to glue the sandbox near the slide if you sweep with a mop or near the bench if you sweep with a broom. For homework, the child takes home the finished page so the homework helper can call out different instructions and the child can point to various objects on the page.

Auditory Processing - Semantic Recall

This section provides activities for children who have difficulty remembering details from a paragraph or story. The child colors and cuts out the small pictures on the page. Then, the therapist/teacher reads the short story for that picture. After reading the story, the child glues the pictures on the page according to the details in the story. For example, on *Tommy's Good Day* pages (pp. 64-65), the child, after listening to the story, must remember to glue his favorite blanket and pillow on his bed, his hat on the top shelf of his closet, and his shoes beside his bed. For homework, the child takes home the finished page to retell the story to someone.

Concepts

This section includes activities for children who have difficulty with responding to and recognizing basic concepts. The child colors and cuts out the small pictures on the page. Then, the therapist/teacher reads each direction from the activities page to prompt the child where to glue each picture. For example, on the *Carnival Time* pages (pp. 110-111), the therapist/teacher reads the first direction which prompts the child to glue two balloons over the roller coaster. After successful completion of this, the therapist continues with the next direction until all items are glued on the page. For homework, the child takes home the finished page to tell where the items were glued.

#BK-307 Say & Glue® for Language & Listening Fun Sheets • ©2003 Super Duper® Publications • www.superduperinc.com • 1-800-277-8737

How To Use This Book

1. The therapist/teacher recognizes a child with language difficulties.

2. The therapist/teacher chooses language goals for the child based on an evaluation.

3. During the initial therapy and/or classroom sessions, the therapist/teacher uses different techniques to teach the concept or language goal.

4. After the child begins to understand the target concept or language goal, it is time to reinforce the skill and teach it through other modalities.

5. Choose an appropriate worksheet for the child, based on his/her goals. These worksheets are designed to target specific goals: categories, functions, auditory processing (following directions and semantic recall), and concepts.

6. The child, following the therapist/teacher's directions, completes the worksheet. During this time, the therapist/teacher gives cues, if needed, to prompt the child or reinforce the earlier skills taught.

7. Then, send the worksheet home with the child for homework. It is also a good idea to send home a copy of the directions page so that the parent/homework helper sees what the child was prompted to do. These pages also include additional language activities that the child practices at home.

8. Parents reinforce the goal at home by reviewing the worksheet, or following through with the additional language activities and extension activities that are offered with the worksheets.

Table of Contents

Categories

Functions

Auditory Processing - Following Complex Directions

#BK-307 Say & Glue® for Language & Listening Fun Sheets • ©2003 Super Duper® Publications • www.superduperinc.com • 1-800-277-8737

Auditory Processing - Following Conditional Directions

Auditory Processing - Semantic Recall

Concepts

Concepts continued

Awards

Parent/Helper Letter

Dear Parents/Homework Helpers,

    Today in speech and language therapy we worked on a fun activity sheet. Please ask your child to do the following checked activities to practice at home.

❏ **Categories**
Name a category and have your child tell you items in that category (e.g., fruit - apple, banana).

❏ **Functions**
Name an item on the sheet and have your child tell what it is used for (e.g., a saw - used for cutting wood). Also, name a function and have him/her tell you what you would use (used to cut wood - a saw).

❏ **Following Complex Directions**
Name two or three items on the page and see if your child can touch all of them in sequential order (e.g., book, apple, desk).

❏ **Following Conditional Directions**
Read an if/then situation to your child and have him/her point to an object (e.g., If you go to school, point to the little snowman. If you don't go to school, point to the big snowman).

❏ **Semantic Recall**
Ask your child to look at the worksheet and re-tell the story to you. Ask different questions about why he/she glued objects where he/she did (e.g., Why did you glue the shoes beside the bed?).

❏ **Concepts**
Have your child tell you where he/she glued the objects (e.g., around the chair, around the umbrella).

❏ **Additional Language Directions**
Ask your child the questions listed under the additional language activities on the directions page.

❏ **Extension Activities**
Help your child participate in the various games and/or activities listed.

Thanks for all of your help. Your work at home helps to reinforce our work at school!

_____   _____
         Teacher   Date

#BK-307 Say & Glue® for Language & Listening Fun Sheets · ©2003 Super Duper® Publications · www.superduperinc.com · 1-800-277-8737

Grocery Store

Directions: Give the child a copy of the picture scene on page 3, and the pictures below. Have the child color and cut out all of the pictures.

Activity: Ask the child to listen carefully. Read the following directions aloud. Put a ✔ in each box to easily track the child's progress.

❑ Find a fruit. Glue it with the other fruits. (apple)

❑ Find a drink. Glue it with the other drinks. (cola)

❑ Find some bread. Glue it with the other bread. (rolls)

❑ Find a dessert. Glue it with the other desserts. (pie)

❑ Find some vegetables. Glue it with the other vegetables. (carrots)

❑ Find some utensils. Glue it with the other utensils. (spoons)

Additional Activities:

1. An apple is a fruit. Name another fruit.

2. Does a lemon taste sweet or sour?

3. Name two kinds of candy.

4. Describe your favorite dessert.

5. How are an orange and a banana different?

Give a copy of the pictures below to the child.

✂

     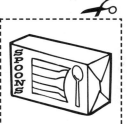

Categories

#BK-307 Say & Glue® for Language & Listening Fun Sheets • ©2003 Super Duper® Publications • www.superduperinc.com • 1-800-277-8737

Grocery Store

Directions: Color and cut out all of the pictures on page 2. Follow the directions to glue those pictures on this picture scene.

#BK-307 Say & Glue® for Language & Listening Fun Sheets · ©2003 Super Duper® Publications · www.superduperinc.com · 1-800-277-8737

Department Store

Directions: Give the child a copy of the picture scene on page 5, and the pictures below. Have the child color and cut out all of the pictures.

Activity: Ask the child to listen carefully. Read the following directions aloud. Put a ✔ in each box to easily track the child's progress.

❏ Find the pieces of clothing. Glue them with the other clothes. (shirt and pants)

❏ Find the furniture. Glue them with the other furniture. (couch and bed)

❏ Find the appliances. Glue them with the other appliances. (blender and toaster)

❏ Find the toys. Glue them with the other toys. (doll and blocks)

❏ Find the shoes. Glue them with the other shoes. (boot and sandal)

❏ Find the things you can read. Glue them with the other things you can read. (book and newspaper)

Additional Activities:

1. Name two kinds of furniture.

2. Name two kinds of clothing.

3. What is the difference between shoes and gloves?

4. What do you do with a toaster?

5. Where can you buy a hat?

Give a copy of the pictures below to the child.

Categories

Department Store

Directions: Color and cut out all of the pictures on page 4. Follow the directions to glue those pictures on this picture scene.

Name

Date

Homework Partner

Categories

Animals

Directions: Give the child a copy of the picture scene on page 7, and the pictures below. Have the child color and cut out all of the pictures.

Activity: Ask the child to listen carefully. Read the following directions aloud. Put a ✔ in each box to easily track the child's progress.

❏ Find the animals that live where it is cold. Glue them in the box with the picture of an igloo. (polar bear and penguin)

❏ Find the farm animals. Glue them in the box with the picture of a barn. (pig and cow)

❏ Find the animals that could be pets. Glue them in the box with the picture of a house. (cat and dog)

❏ Find the zoo animals. Glue them in the box with the picture of a zoo. (monkey and giraffe)

❏ Find the animals that live in the desert. Glue them in the box with the picture of the desert. (camel and rattlesnake)

❏ Find the animals that live in the ocean. Glue them in the box with the picture of the beach. (octopus and starfish)

Additional Activities:

1. Name something you see on a farm.

2. What can you get from a cow?

3. Describe a pet you would like.

4. Name an animal that lives in the water.

- -
Give a copy of the pictures below to the child.

Categories

#BK-307 Say & Glue® for Language & Listening Fun Sheets • ©2003 Super Duper® Publications • www.superduperinc.com • 1-800-277-8737

Animals

Directions: Color and cut out all of the pictures on page 6. Follow the directions to glue those pictures on this picture scene.

_____   _____   _____   **Categories**
Homework Partner   Date   Name

Bedroom

Directions: Give the child a copy of the picture scene on page 9, and the pictures below. Have the child color and cut out all of the pictures.

Activity: Ask the child to listen carefully. Read the following directions aloud. Put a ✔ in each box to easily track the child's progress.

❏ Find the clothes. Glue them on the bed. (dress and hat)

❏ Find the toys. Glue them on the shelf. (yoyo and car)

❏ Find the furniture. Glue them next to the door. (nightstand and chair)

❏ Find the animals. Glue them on the rug. (cat and dog)

❏ Find the food. Glue it in the basket. (apple and chips)

❏ Find the books. Glue them on the floor. (coloring book and novel)

Additional Activities:

1. Describe your bedroom.

2. What is the difference between pants and a shirt?

3. Tell about a game you play in your room.

4. Name a piece of furniture in your room.

5. Name two toys.

Give a copy of the pictures below to the child.

Categories

#BK-307 Say & Glue® for Language & Listening Fun Sheets · ©2003 Super Duper® Publications · www.superduperinc.com · 1-800-277-8737

Bedroom

Directions: Color and cut out all of the pictures on page 8. Follow the directions to glue those pictures on this picture scene.

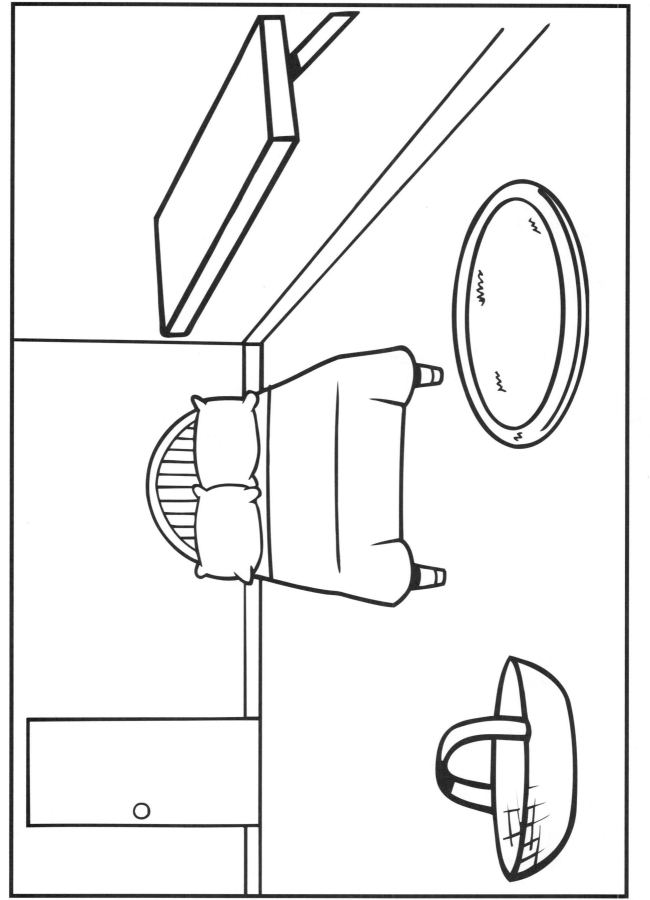

Name

Date

Homework Partner

Categories

Extension Activities for Categories

Extension activities give the therapist/teacher and parent an opportunity to reinforce the target skills at home and school.

1. When shopping at the grocery store, talk about the category of each item as you place it in the buggy (e.g., fruit, dessert, meat).

2. Look through magazines and newspaper ads. Have the child cut out pictures and put them in stacks according to category (e.g., clothes, food).

3. Play a "find and seek" game. Name a category, such as "toy," and have the child look around and name items they see in that category.

4. Expand the "find and seek" game by having the child name the category. You name items you see and let them decide if it belongs in that category.

5. Have child sort common object cards into categories.

6. Make a "category collage." Have newspapers, magazines, and catalogs available to cut pictures from. Sort the pictures by category (clothes, food, etc.) and glue each category on a sheet of paper.

7. Name a category and have child draw pictures of items in that category.

8. Name various items in a category (e.g., apple, orange, banana). Have child guess the name of the category (fruits).

Tool Shed

Directions: Give the child a copy of the picture scene on page 13, and the pictures below. Have the child color and cut out all of the pictures.

Activity: Ask the child to listen carefully. Read the following directions aloud. Put a ✔ in each box to easily track the child's progress.

❏ Find something you could use to cut wood. Glue it on your page. (saw)

❏ Find something you could use to cut the grass. Glue it on your page. (lawn mower)

❏ Find something you could use to gather leaves. Glue it on your page. (rake)

❏ Find something you could use to dig a hole. Glue it on your page. (shovel)

❏ Find something you could use to put dirt in. Glue it on your page. (wheelbarrow)

❏ Find something you could use to cut the bushes. Glue it on your page. (trimmers)

Additional Activities:

1. What is the difference between a saw and a lawn mower?

2. What do you use a shovel for?

3. Name something you can put in a wheelbarrow.

4. Why do you need to cut the grass?

5. Name something a saw can cut.

- -
Give a copy of the pictures below to the child.

     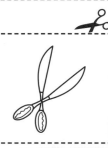

Functions

Tool Shed

Directions: Color and cut out all of the pictures on page 12. Follow the directions to glue those pictures on this picture scene.

Grocery Store

Directions: Give the child a copy of the picture scene on page 15, and the pictures below. Have the child color and cut out all of the pictures.

Activity: Ask the child to listen carefully. Read the following directions aloud. Put a ✔ in each box to easily track the child's progress.

❑ Find something you could pour in a cup. Glue it on your page. (milk)

❑ Find something you could read. Glue it on your page. (book)

❑ Find something you could cook on a grill. Glue it on your page. (steak)

❑ Find something you could eat on a salad. Glue it on your page. (lettuce)

❑ Find something you could use to eat cereal. Glue it on your page. (spoon)

❑ Find something you could feed to a dog. Glue it on your page. (bone)

Additional Activities:

1. Tell about a time you went to the grocery store.

2. Name something cold at the grocery store.

3. What is the difference between a cup and a plate?

4. Can you buy a couch at the grocery store?

5. Name two vegetables.

Give a copy of the pictures below to the child.

  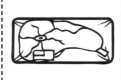   

Functions

#BK-307 Say & Glue® for Language & Listening Fun Sheets • ©2003 Super Duper® Publications • www.superduperinc.com • 1-800-277-8737

Grocery Store

Directions: Color and cut out all of the pictures on page 14. Follow the directions to glue those pictures on this picture scene.

Name

Date

Homework Partner

Schoolroom

Directions: Give the child a copy of the picture scene on page 17, and the pictures below. Have the child color and cut out all of the pictures.

Activity: Ask the child to listen carefully. Read the following directions aloud. Put a ✔ in each box to easily track the child's progress.

❑ Find something you write on. Glue it on your page. (paper)

❑ Find something you write with. Glue it on your page. (pencil)

❑ Find something you use to cut paper. Glue it on your page. (scissors)

❑ Find something you use to make paper stick together. Glue it on your page. (glue)

❑ Find something you read. Glue it on your page. (book)

❑ Find something you use to take writing off the board. Glue it on your page. (eraser)

Additional Activities:

1. Do animals go to school?

2. Describe your favorite teacher.

3. Tell two things you do in P.E. class.

4. Name something a teacher uses.

5. Why does a school have a principal?

Give a copy of the pictures below to the child.

Functions

#BK-307 Say & Glue® for Language & Listening Fun Sheets • ©2003 Super Duper® Publications • www.superduperinc.com • 1-800-277-8737

Schoolroom

Directions: Color and cut out all of the pictures on page 16. Follow the directions to glue those pictures on this picture scene.

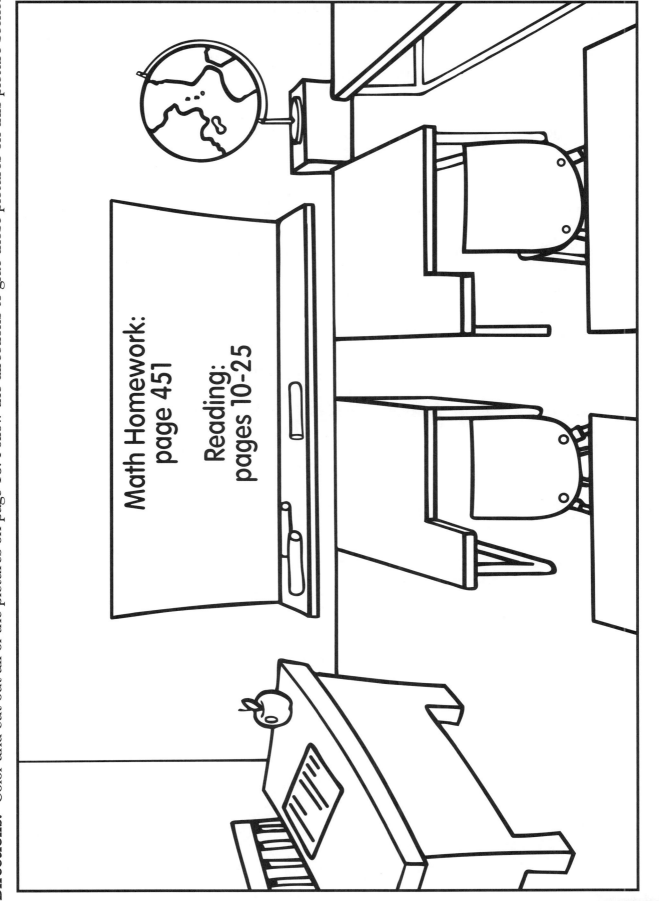

Math Homework:
page 451

Reading:
pages 10-25

Name _____

Date _____

Homework Partner _____

Bathroom

Directions: Give the child a copy of the picture scene on page 19, and the pictures below. Have the child color and cut out all of the pictures.

Activity: Ask the child to listen carefully. Read the following directions aloud. Put a ✔ in each box to easily track the child's progress.

❏ Find something you use to brush your hair. Glue it on your page. (brush)

❏ Find something you put on a toothbrush. Glue it on your page. (toothpaste)

❏ Find something you use to wash your face. Glue it on your page. (washcloth)

❏ Find something you use to cut your fingernails. Glue it on your page. (clippers)

❏ Find something you use to shave. Glue it on your page. (razor)

❏ Find something you use to see yourself. Glue it on your page. (mirror)

Additional Activities:

1. What is the difference between a hairbrush and a toothbrush?

2. Do you need soap to take a bath?

3. What do you need to wash your face?

4. What is the difference between a bath and a shower?

5. Name one more thing you find in a bathroom.

Give a copy of the pictures below to the child.

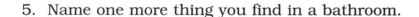

Functions

Bathroom

Directions: Color and cut out all of the pictures on page 18. Follow the directions to glue those pictures on this picture scene.

Homework Partner   Date   Name

Kitchen

Directions: Give the child a copy of the picture scene on page 21, and the pictures below. Have the child color and cut out all of the pictures.

Activity: Ask the child to listen carefully. Read the following directions aloud. Put a ✔ in each box to easily track the child's progress.

❑ Find something you use to cook. Glue it on your page. (pot)

❑ Find something you tell time with. Glue it on your page. (clock)

❑ Find something you use to cut things with. Glue it on your page. (knife)

❑ Find something you use to make a sandwich. Glue it on your page. (bread)

❑ Find something you use to put a drink in. Glue it on your page. (cup)

❑ Find something you use to keep things cold. Glue it on your page. (ice)

Additional Activities:

1. Describe your favorite meal.

2. Name two things in your kitchen.

3. Tell about a time you helped cook something.

4. What is a refrigerator used for?

5. What is the difference between a spoon and a knife?

Give a copy of the pictures below to the child.

Functions

#BK-307 Say & Glue® for Language & Listening Fun Sheets • ©2003 Super Duper® Publications • www.superduperinc.com • 1-800-277-8737

Kitchen

Directions: Color and cut out all of the pictures on page 20. Follow the directions to glue those pictures on this picture scene.

Homework Partner   Date   Name   **Functions**

Bedroom

Directions: Give the child a copy of the picture scene on page 23, and the pictures below. Have the child color and cut out all of the pictures.

Activity: Ask the child to listen carefully. Read the following directions aloud. Put a ✔ in each box to easily track the child's progress.

❏ Find something you wear on your feet. Glue them on your page. (shoes)

❏ Find something you put on the floor. Glue it on your page. (rug)

❏ Find something you play with. Glue it on your page. (blocks)

❏ Find something you put on your bed. Glue it on your page. (pillow)

❏ Find something you sit in. Glue it on your page. (chair)

❏ Find something you turn on when it's dark. Glue it on your page. (lamp)

Additional Activities:

1. Describe your bedspread.

2. What do you do with a blanket?

3. Name something on your dresser.

4. What is a nightstand used for?

5. Name something in your closet.

Give a copy of the pictures below to the child.

 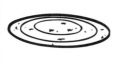  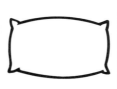  

Functions

#BK-307 Say & Glue® for Language & Listening Fun Sheets • ©2003 Super Duper® Publications • www.superduperinc.com • 1-800-277-8737

Bedroom

Directions: Color and cut out all of the pictures on page 22. Follow the directions to glue those pictures on this picture scene.

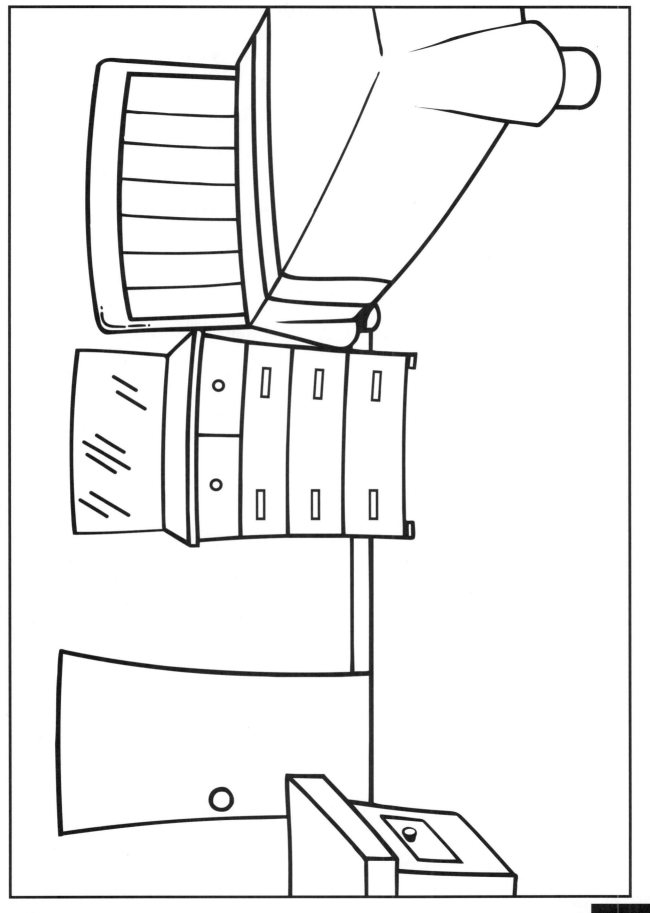

Name

Date

Homework Partner

#BK-307 Say & Glue® for Language & Listening Fun Sheets • ©2003 Super Duper® Publications • www.superduperinc.com • 1-800-277-8737

Garage

Directions: Give the child a copy of the picture scene on page 25, and the pictures below. Have the child color and cut out all of the pictures.

Activity: Ask the child to listen carefully. Read the following directions aloud. Put a ✔ in each box to easily track the child's progress.

❏ Find something you can ride. Glue it on your page. (bicycle)

❏ Find something you use to paint. Glue it on your page. (paintbrush)

❏ Find something you use to sweep. Glue it on your page. (broom)

❏ Find something you use to hit a ball. Glue it on your page. (bat)

❏ Find something you can put things in and pull. Glue it on your page. (wagon)

❏ Find something you use in a pool. Glue it on your page. (float)

Additional Activities:

1. What do you do with a paintbrush?

2. Can you paint a wall?

3. Why do you sweep the floor?

4. How is a garage different from a kitchen?

5. Name three other things that are kept in a garage.

Give a copy of the pictures below to the child.

Functions

#BK-307 Say & Glue® for Language & Listening Fun Sheets • ©2003 Super Duper® Publications • www.superduperinc.com • 1-800-277-8737

Garage

Directions: Color and cut out all of the pictures on page 24. Follow the directions to glue those pictures on this picture scene.

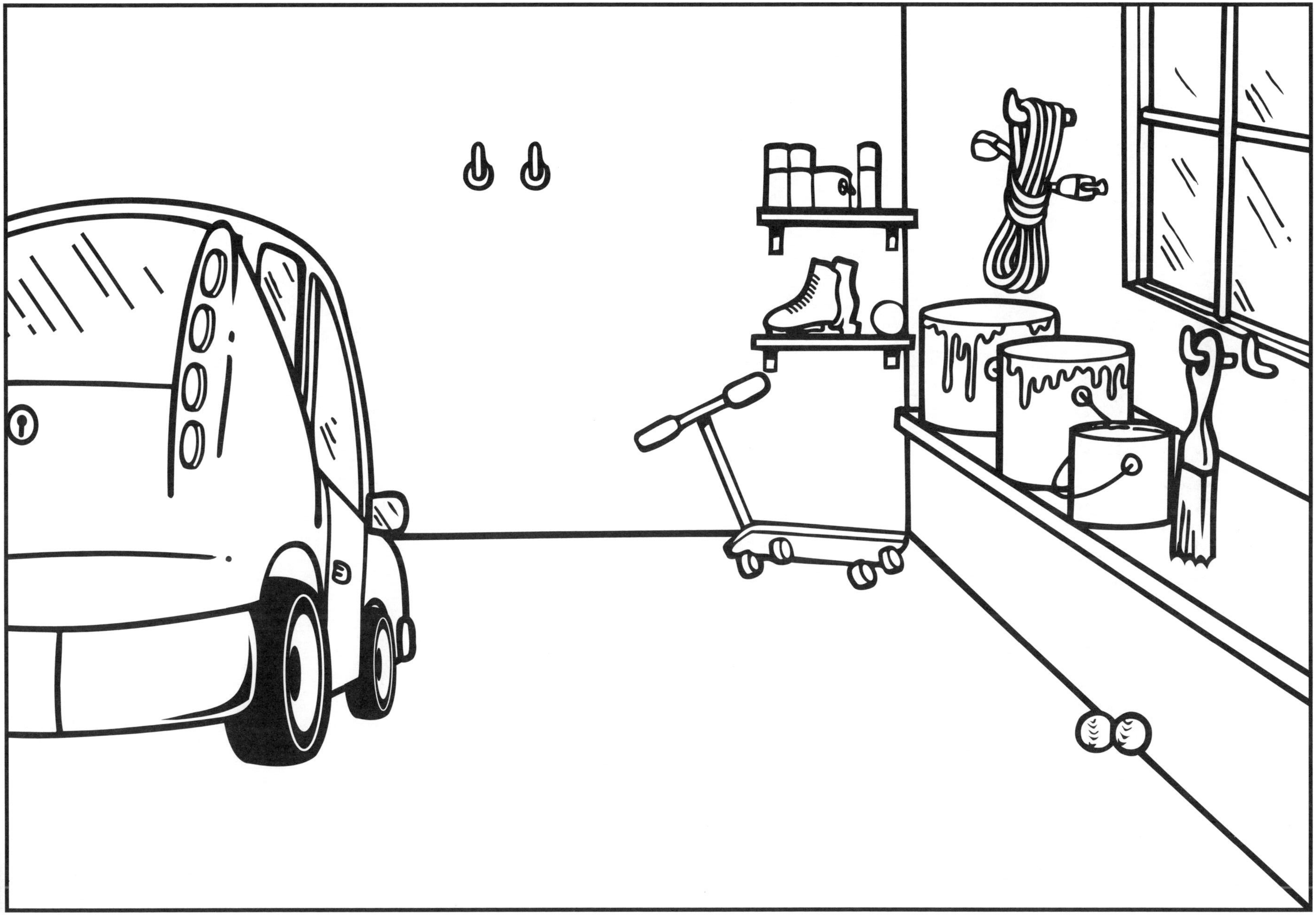

Name _____

Date _____

Homework Partner _____

Extension Activities for Functions

Extension activities give the therapist and parent an opportunity to reinforce the target skills at home and school.

1. As you pick up and clean around the house, ask the child what various objects are used for (e.g., shoe, spoon, book).

2. Tell the child a job that needs to be done (e.g., washing dishes) and ask them to name the items you would need to do that job.

3. When in a store, ask the child what various objects are used for (e.g., knife, pen, ball).

4. Have the child look at common object cards and name the function of the objects.

5. Put various objects into a bag. Have the child pull an object out of the bag and tell what it is used for.

6. Name a job (e.g., cutting grass) and have the child draw pictures of objects needed to do that job.

#BK-307 Say & Glue® for Language & Listening Fun Sheets • ©2003 Super Duper® Publications • www.superduperinc.com • 1-800-277-8737

AUDITORY PROCESSING:

Following Complex Directions
Following Conditional Directions
Semantic Recall

Bedroom

Directions: Give the child a copy of the picture scene on page 29, and the pictures below. Have the child color and cut out all of the pictures.

Activity: Ask the child to listen carefully. Read the following directions aloud. Put a ✔ in each box to easily track the child's progress.

❏ Find the lamp and the shoes. Glue the lamp on the nightstand and the shoes in the closet.

❏ Find the rug and the brush. Glue the rug in front of the chair and the brush on the dresser.

❏ Find the car and the pillow. Glue the car next to the dresser and the pillow on the floor next to the bed.

❏ Find the shirt and the blocks. Glue the shirt on the bed and the blocks in the closet.

❏ Find the book and the hat. Glue the book on the bed and the hat in the closet.

❏ Find the ball and the doll. Glue the ball on the floor and the doll on the chair.

Additional Activities:

1. What do you do with a lamp?

2. Is a pillow hard or soft?

3. Where do you put a rug?

4. Does a bedroom have a door?

Give a copy of the pictures below to the child.

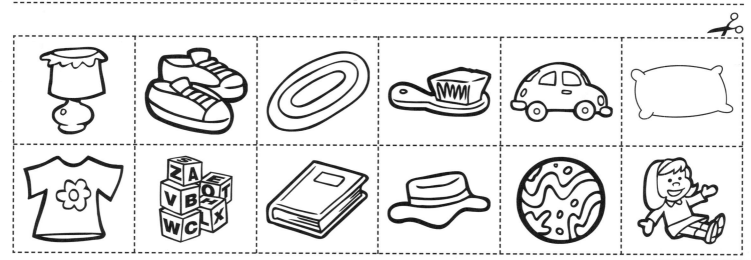

#BK-307 Say & Glue® for Language & Listening Fun Sheets · ©2003 Super Duper® Publications · www.superduperinc.com · 1-800-277-8737

Complex Directions

Bedroom

Directions: Color and cut out all of the pictures on page 28. Follow the directions to glue those pictures on this picture scene.

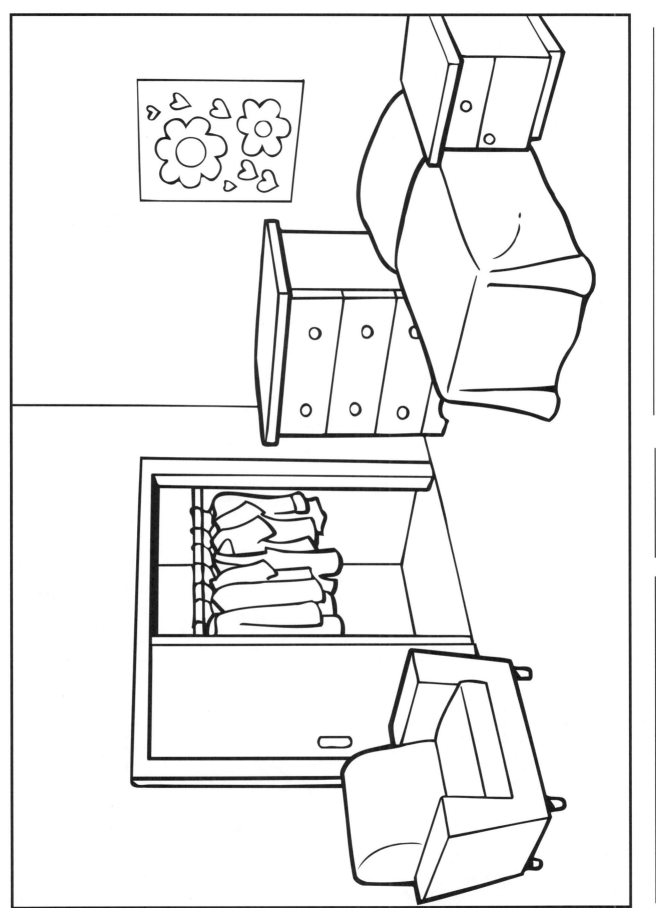

Complex Directions

29

#BK-307 Say & Glue® for Language & Listening Fun Sheets • ©2003 Super Duper® Publications • www.superduperinc.com • 1-800-277-8737

Classroom

Directions: Give the child a copy of the picture scene on page 31, and the pictures below. Have the child color and cut out all of the pictures.

Activity: Ask the child to listen carefully. Read the following directions aloud. Put a ✔ in each box to easily track the child's progress.

❏ Find the book and the apple. Glue the book on the floor and the apple on the teacher's desk.

❏ Find the eraser and the pencil. Glue the eraser by the board and the pencil on a desk.

❏ Find the chair and the desk. Glue the chair in front of the computer and the desk in front of the window.

❏ Find the paper and the person. Glue the paper on a desk and the person beside the aquarium.

❏ Find the hat and the lunchbox. Glue the hat on the person and the lunchbox on a desk.

❏ Find the ball and the fish. Glue the ball under the window and the fish in the aquarium.

Additional Activities:

1. Why do you need an eraser on a pencil?

2. How are a marker and a pencil different?

3. Name something you can pack in a lunchbox.

4. What is the difference between a desk and a chair?

Give a copy of the pictures below to the child.

Complex Directions

#BK-307 Say & Glue® for Language & Listening Fun Sheets · ©2003 Super Duper® Publications · www.superduperinc.com · 1-800-277-8737

Classroom

Directions: Color and cut out all of the pictures on page 30. Follow the directions to glue those pictures on this picture scene.

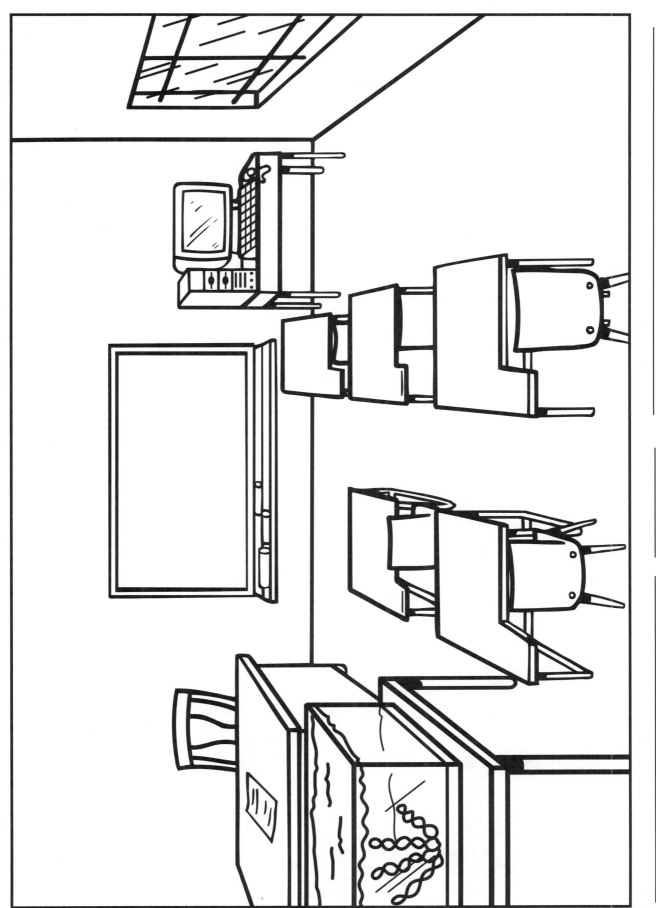

Name _____

Date _____

Homework Partner _____

City Street

Directions: Give the child a copy of the picture scene on page 33, and the pictures below. Have the child color and cut out all of the pictures.

Activity: Ask the child to listen carefully. Read the following directions aloud. Put a ✔ in each box to easily track the child's progress.

❏ Find the stop sign and the car. Glue the car on the road and the stop sign in front of it.

❏ Find the bench and the bird. Glue the bench next to the tree and the bird over the sun.

❏ Find the dog and the apple. Glue the dog on the empty side of the street and the apple under the tree.

❏ Find the person and the airplane. Glue the person in front of a store and the airplane over a building.

❏ Find the bike and the ball. Glue the bike on the road and the ball beside the tree.

❏ Find the box and the bag. Glue the box in front of a store and the bag beside the person.

Additional Activities:

1. Why do you need stop signs?

2. Who flies an airplane?

3. Name something you can ride on the street.

4. What do you do with a bench?

Give a copy of the pictures below to the child. ✀

Complex Directions

#BK-307 Say & Glue® for Language & Listening Fun Sheets • ©2003 Super Duper® Publications • www.superduperinc.com • 1-800-277-8737

City Street

Directions: Color and cut out all of the pictures on page 32. Follow the directions to glue those pictures on this picture scene.

Name

Date

Homework Partner

Complex Directions

33

Camp-Out

Directions: Give the child a copy of the picture scene on page 35, and the pictures below. Have the child color and cut out all of the pictures.

Activity: Ask the child to listen carefully. Read the following directions aloud. Put a ✔ in each box to easily track the child's progress.

- ❏ Find the chair and the thermos. Glue the chair next to the tent and the thermos near the fire.

- ❏ Find the bench and the smoke. Glue the bench beside the table and the smoke over the fire.

- ❏ Find the lantern and the bike. Glue the lantern on the table and the bike beside the chair.

- ❏ Find the hammock and the fishing pole. Glue the hammock between the trees and the fishing pole near the table.

- ❏ Find the tent and the bird. Glue the tent next to the table and the bird in a tree.

- ❏ Find the cooler and the football. Glue the cooler beside the table and the football beside a tree.

Additional Activities:

1. How are a tent and a house different?

2. Name something you take camping.

3. What is a lantern used for?

4. What do you do with a hammock?

5. How do you catch a fish?

Give a copy of the pictures below to the child.

Complex Directions

#BK-307 Say & Glue® for Language & Listening Fun Sheets • ©2003 Super Duper® Publications • www.superduperinc.com • 1-800-277-8737

Camp-Out

Directions: Color and cut out all of the pictures on page 34. Follow the directions to glue those pictures on this picture scene.

Name

Date

Homework Partner

Complex Directions

#BK-307 Say & Glue® for Language & Listening Fun Sheets • ©2003 Super Duper® Publications • www.superduperinc.com • 1-800-277-8737

Kitchen

Directions: Give the child a copy of the picture scene on page 37, and the pictures below. Have the child color and cut out all of the pictures.

Activity: Ask the child to listen carefully. Read the following directions aloud. Put a ✔ in each box to easily track the child's progress.

❏ Find the dishes and the flowers. Glue the dishes beside the sink and the flowers on the table.

❏ Find the pot and the clock. Glue the pot beside the stove and the clock over the refrigerator.

❏ Find the rug and the silverware. Glue the rug on the floor in front of the sink and the silverware on the table.

❏ Find the fruit bowl and the note. Glue the fruit bowl on the counter and the note on the refrigerator.

❏ Find the cup and the plate. Glue the cup on the table and the plate on the counter.

❏ Find the apple and the sponge. Glue the apple beside the fruit bowl and the sponge beside the sink.

Additional Activities:

1. Why do you water flowers?

2. Name something you can cook in a pot.

3. What do you need to wash dishes?

4. What is the difference between a refrigerator and a freezer?

5. What do you do with a clock?

Give a copy of the pictures below to the child.

Complex Directions

#BK-307 Say & Glue® for Language & Listening Fun Sheets · ©2003 Super Duper® Publications · www.superduperinc.com · 1-800-277-8737

Kitchen

Directions: Color and cut out all of the pictures on page 36. Follow the directions to glue those pictures on this picture scene.

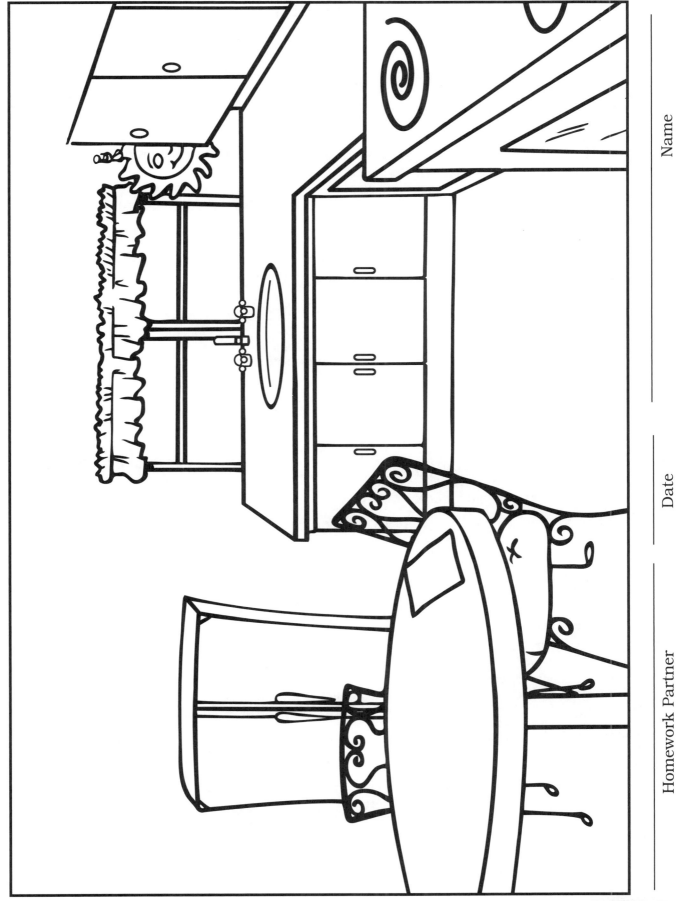

Name _____

Date _____

Homework Partner _____

Cook-Out

Directions: Give the child a copy of the picture scene on page 39, and the pictures below. Have the child color and cut out all of the pictures.

Activity: Ask the child to listen carefully. Read the following directions aloud. Put a ✔ in each box to easily track the child's progress.

❑ Find the hamburger patties and the hot dogs. Glue the patties on the grill and the hot dogs on the plate on the table.

❑ Find the float and the ball. Glue the float by the pool and the ball beside the chair.

❑ Find the mustard and ketchup. Glue the mustard by the grill and the ketchup on the table.

❑ Find the chair and the towel. Glue the chair beside the pool and the towel on one of the chairs.

❑ Find the cooler and the chips. Glue the cooler beside the grill and the chips on the table.

❑ Find the spatula and the cup. Glue the spatula on the grill and the cup beside the pool.

Additional Activities:

1. Name something you cook on a grill.
2. What is a game you can play in the pool?
3. Name something you put on a hot dog.
4. Do you get wet in a pool?
5. What would you do with a towel at the pool?

Give a copy of the pictures below to the child.

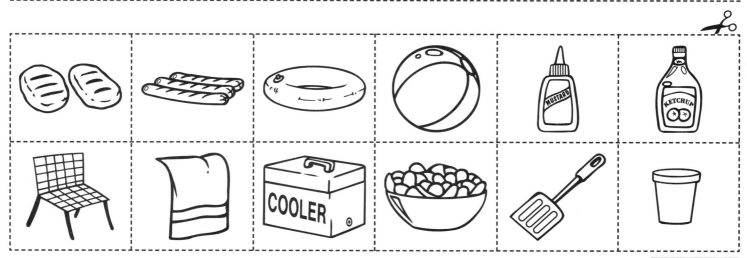

Complex Directions

#BK-307 Say & Glue® for Language & Listening Fun Sheets • ©2003 Super Duper® Publications • www.superduperinc.com • 1-800-277-8737

Directions: Color and cut out all of the pictures on page 38. Follow the directions to glue those pictures on this picture scene.

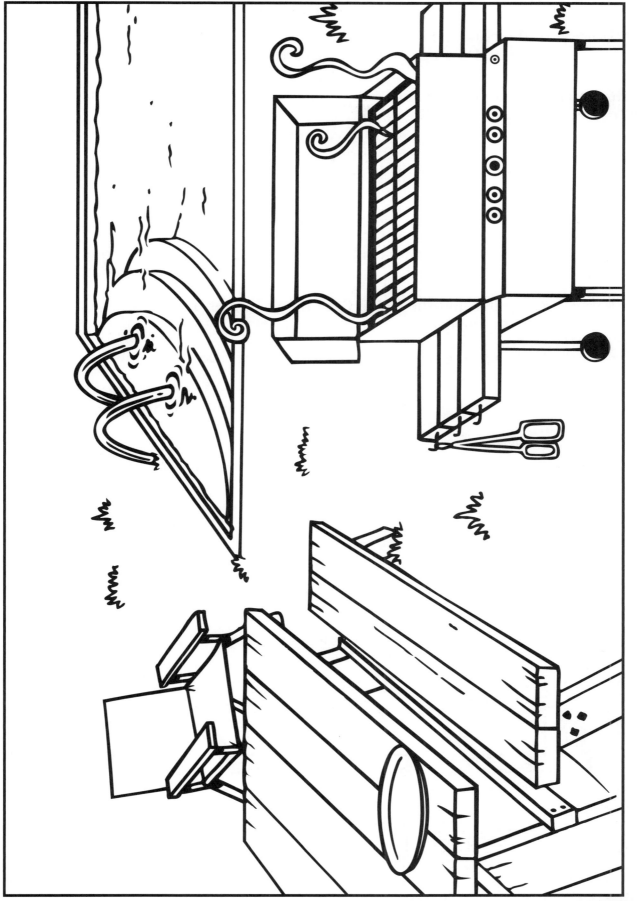

Name

Date

Homework Partner

Library

Directions: Give the child a copy of the picture scene on page 41, and the pictures below. Have the child color and cut out all of the pictures.

Activity: Ask the child to listen carefully. Read the following directions aloud. Put a ✔ in each box to easily track the child's progress.

❏ Find one chair and a book. Glue the chair next to a table and the book on a shelf.

❏ Find two more books. Glue one book on a table and one on the floor.

❏ Find a magazine and another chair. Glue the magazine on top of the television and the chair under a table.

❏ Find the computer and the globe. Glue the computer on a table and the globe on top of a bookcase.

❏ Find the table and the newspaper. Glue the table next to a shelf and the newspaper on a shelf.

❏ Find the boy and the girl. Glue the boy next to a table and the girl near a shelf.

Additional Activities:

1. What can you do at a library?
2. Can you buy food at a library?
3. What do you need to watch a movie?
4. What do you do with a book?
5. Why should you be quiet in a library?

Give a copy of the pictures below to the child.

Oops! 😮

We made an error on this page. Please go to **www.superduperinc.com/sayGlue307** to download a corrected page.

Complex Directions

#BK-307 Say & Glue® for Language & Listening Fun Sheets • ©2003 Super Duper® Publications • www.superduperinc.com • 1-800-277-8737

Library

Directions: Color and cut out all of the pictures on page 40. Follow the directions to glue those pictures on this picture scene.

Homework Partner   Date   Name

41

#BK-307 Say & Glue® for Language & Listening Fun Sheets • ©2003 Super Duper® Publications • www.superduperinc.com • 1-800-277-8737

Zoo

Directions: Give the child a copy of the picture scene on page 43, and the pictures below. Have the child color and cut out all of the pictures.

Activity: Ask the child to listen carefully. Read the following directions aloud. Put a ✔ in each box to easily track the child's progress.

❏ Find two people. Glue one next to the water and the other one beside the tree.

❏ Find the turtle and the bird. Glue the turtle on the rock and the bird in the tree.

❏ Find the fish and the snake. Glue the fish in the water and the snake by the bench.

❏ Find the elephant and the giraffe. Glue the elephant in the fence and the giraffe under the tree.

❏ Find the hay and the bird's nest. Glue the hay near the elephant and the nest in the tree.

❏ Find the lion and seal. Glue the lion near the elephant and the seal in the water.

Additional Activities:

1. Name an animal that lives in the water.

2. What is the difference between a bird and a turtle?

3. Describe a snake.

4. Name an animal that can climb a tree.

5. Which is bigger, an elephant or a tiger?

Give a copy of the pictures below to the child.

✂

Complex Directions

#BK-307 Say & Glue® for Language & Listening Fun Sheets • ©2003 Super Duper® Publications • www.superduperinc.com • 1-800-277-8737

Zoo

Directions: Color and cut out all of the pictures on page 42. Follow the directions to glue those pictures on this picture scene.

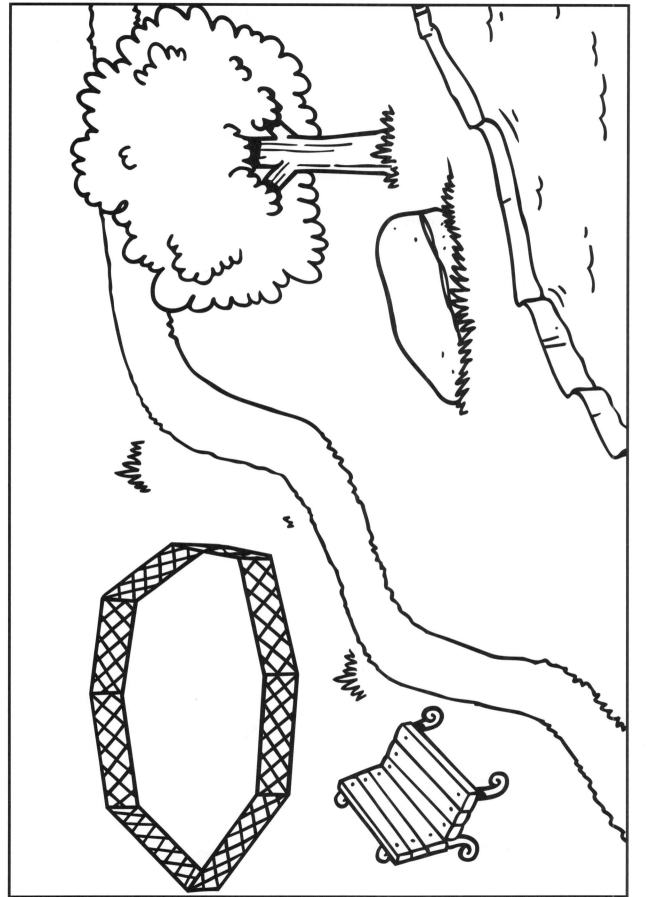

Name _____

Date _____

Homework Partner _____

Halloween

Directions: Give the child a copy of the picture scene on page 45, and the pictures below. Have the child color and cut out all of the pictures.

Activity: Ask the child to listen carefully. Read the following directions aloud. Put a ✔ in each box to easily track the child's progress.

❏ Find the bat and the jack-o'-lantern. Glue the bat under the moon and the jack-o'-lantern in front of the house.

❏ Find the two pieces of candy. Glue one beside the person dressed as a witch and the other under the tree.

❏ Find the cat and the skeleton. Glue the cat beside the house and the skeleton under the tree.

❏ Find the mask and the smoke. Glue the mask on the boy and the smoke over the chimney.

❏ Find the stars and the basket. Glue the stars near the moon and the basket by the person dressed as a witch.

❏ Find the apple and the clown. Glue the apple on the tree and the clown beside the person dressed as a ghost.

Additional Activities:

1. What do people do at Halloween?

2. What type of food do children get when they trick-or-treat?

3. Describe a ghost costume.

4. Where do you wear a mask?

Give a copy of the pictures below to the child.

Complex Directions

#BK-307 Say & Glue® for Language & Listening Fun Sheets • ©2003 Super Duper® Publications • www.superduperinc.com • 1-800-277-8737

Halloween

Directions: Color and cut out all of the pictures on page 44. Follow the directions to glue those pictures on this picture scene.

Homework Partner   Date   Name

45

#BK-307 Say & Glue® for Language & Listening Fun Sheets • ©2003 Super Duper® Publications • www.superduperinc.com • 1-800-277-8737

Winter Day

Directions: Give the child a copy of the picture scene on page 47, and the pictures below. Have the child color and cut out all of the pictures.

Activity: Ask the child to listen carefully. Read the following directions aloud. Put a ✔ in each box to easily track the child's progress.

❏ If a cat can climb a tree, glue the hat on the big snowman. If a cat can't climb a tree, glue the hat on the little snowman.

❏ If you can write with a pencil, glue the bird on the little tree. If you can't write with a pencil, glue the bird on the big tree.

❏ If a baby can go to school, glue the carrot nose on the little snowman. If a baby can't go to school, glue the carrot nose on the big snowman.

❏ If your shoe is bigger than a penny, glue the sled beside the big tree. If your shoe is smaller than a penny, glue the sled beside the little tree.

❏ If you take a bath in milk, glue the boy on the sled. If you take a bath in water, glue the boy beside a snowman.

❏ If snow is hot, glue the dog beside a snowman. If snow is cold, glue the dog beside a tree.

Additional Activities:

1. Tell about a time you played in the snow.

2. Describe what snow feels like.

3. How do you make a snowman?

4. What do you wear to go out in the snow?

5. What do you do with a sled?

Give a copy of the pictures below to the child.

Conditional Directions

#BK-307 Say & Glue® for Language & Listening Fun Sheets • ©2003 Super Duper® Publications • www.superduperinc.com • 1-800-277-8737

Winter Day

Directions: Color and cut out all of the pictures on page 46. Follow the directions to glue those pictures on this picture scene.

Conditional Directions

Birthday Party

Directions: Give the child a copy of the picture scene on page 49, and the pictures below. Have the child color and cut out all of the pictures.

Activity: Ask the child to listen carefully. Read the following directions aloud. Put a ✔ in each box to easily track the child's progress.

❏ If you use a brush to fix your hair, glue the chair beside the long table. If you use a shoe to fix your hair, glue the chair beside the round table.

❏ If you can drive a chair, glue the hat on the boy. If you can't drive a chair, glue the hat on the girl.

❏ If you can walk on a bridge, glue the horn on the chair. If you can't walk on a bridge, glue the horn on the floor.

❏ If you eat soup with a spoon, glue the banner on the window. If you eat soup with a fork, glue the banner on the front of the table.

❏ If you use scissors to cut the grass, glue the present on the round table. If you use a lawn mower to cut the grass, glue the present on the long table.

❏ If a dog can bark, glue the cake on the round table. If a dog can't bark, glue the cake on the long table.

Additional Activities:

1. What do you put on top of a birthday cake?

2. Name two games you play at a birthday party.

3. What do you use to eat ice cream?

4. How can you light the candles on a cake?

5. Tell about one of your birthday parties.

Give a copy of the pictures below to the child.

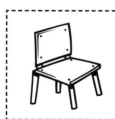  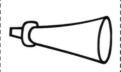   

Conditional Directions

#BK-307 Say & Glue® for Language & Listening Fun Sheets • ©2003 Super Duper® Publications • www.superduperinc.com • 1-800-277-8737

Birthday Party

Directions: Color and cut out all of the pictures on page 48. Follow the directions to glue those pictures on this picture scene.

Farm

Directions: Give the child a copy of the picture scene on page 51, and the pictures below. Have the child color and cut out all of the pictures.

Activity: Ask the child to listen carefully. Read the following directions aloud. Put a ✔ in each box to easily track the child's progress.

❑ If ice cream is cold, glue the basket of eggs near the barn. If ice cream is hot, glue the basket of eggs near the pond.

❑ If a duck can swim, glue the pig near the other pig. If a duck can't swim, glue the pig near the barn.

❑ If a chair has a motor, glue the dog near the pond. If a chair doesn't have a motor, glue the dog near the field.

❑ If you take a bath in a cup, glue the horse near the barn. If you take a bath in a tub, glue the horse in the field.

❑ If fire will burn, glue the duck in the pond. If fire won't burn, glue the duck in the field.

❑ If you use a desk at school, glue the cow in the field. If you don't use a desk at school, glue the cow near the pigs.

Additional Activities:

1. What can you get from a chicken?

2. Name something a farmer can plant.

3. What lives in a barn?

4. Tell something a farmer does.

5. What is the difference between a pig and a dog?

Give a copy of the pictures below to the child.

Conditional Directions

#BK-307 Say & Glue® for Language & Listening Fun Sheets • ©2003 Super Duper® Publications • www.superduperinc.com • 1-800-277-8737

Farm

Directions: Color and cut out all of the pictures on page 50. Follow the directions to glue those pictures on this picture scene.

Name _____

Date _____

Homework Partner _____

#BK-307 Say & Glue® for Language & Listening Fun Sheets • ©2003 Super Duper® Publications • www.superduperinc.com • 1-800-277-8737

Beach

Directions: Give the child a copy of the picture scene on page 53, and the pictures below. Have the child color and cut out all of the pictures.

Activity: Ask the child to listen carefully. Read the following directions aloud. Put a ✔ in each box to easily track the child's progress.

❏ If a fish can live out of water, glue the picnic basket under the umbrella. If a fish can't live out of water, glue the picnic basket on the blanket.

❏ If you sleep in a bed, glue the chair near the umbrella. If you sleep on a table, glue the chair near the blanket.

❏ If a chair has hair, glue the surfboard on the sand. If a chair doesn't have hair, glue the surfboard in the water.

❏ If you read a book, glue the bucket near the water. If you don't read a book, glue the bucket near the crab.

❏ If a bicycle has three wheels, glue the shovel under the umbrella. If a bicycle has two wheels, glue the shovel near the bucket.

❏ If you can cut paper, glue the radio under the umbrella. If you can't cut paper, glue the radio on the blanket.

Additional Activities:

1. What is something you bring to the beach?

2. Name two animals that live in the ocean.

3. Does a seagull fly?

4. Can you swim at the beach?

5. What do you do with a raft at the beach?

Give a copy of the pictures below to the child.

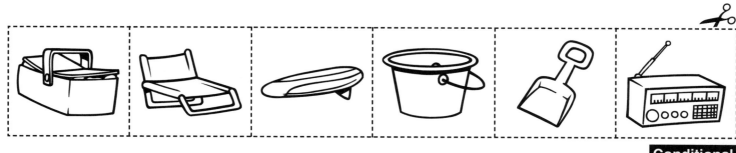

Conditional Directions

#BK-307 Say & Glue® for Language & Listening Fun Sheets • ©2003 Super Duper® Publications • www.superduperinc.com • 1-800-277-8737

Beach

Directions: Color and cut out all of the pictures on page 52. Follow the directions to glue those pictures on this picture scene.

Name

Date

Homework Partner

Conditional Directions

53

Picnic

Directions: Give the child a copy of the picture scene on page 55, and the pictures below. Have the child color and cut out all of the pictures.

Activity: Ask the child to listen carefully. Read the following directions aloud. Put a ✔ in each box to easily track the child's progress.

❏ If you put gas in a car, glue the apple on the tree. If you put juice in a car, glue the apple under the tree.

❏ If dogs can climb trees, glue the chair by the blanket. If dogs can't climb trees, glue the chair by the lake.

❏ If a dime is money, glue the bat and ball by the blanket. If a dime is a toy, glue the bat and ball by the lake.

❏ If you play soccer with a helmet, glue the can on the blanket. If you play football with a helmet, glue the can on the table.

❏ If a tree is made of wood, glue the sandwich on the blanket. If a tree is made of rubber, glue the sandwich on the table.

❏ If you can tear a piece of paper, glue the watermelon on the blanket. If you can't tear a piece of paper, glue the watermelon on the table.

Additional Activities:

1. Name a food you can take on a picnic.

2. Grapes are a fruit. Name another fruit.

3. What game do you play with a bat and ball?

4. Tell about a time when you went on a picnic.

5. What is your favorite food?

Give a copy of the pictures below to the child.

#BK-307 Say & Glue® for Language & Listening Fun Sheets · ©2003 Super Duper® Publications · www.superduperinc.com · 1-800-277-8737

Picnic

Directions: Color and cut out all of the pictures on page 54. Follow the directions to glue those pictures on this picture scene.

Homework Partner   Date   Name

Circus

Directions: Give the child a copy of the picture scene on page 57, and the pictures below. Have the child color and cut out all of the pictures.

Activity: Ask the child to listen carefully. Read the following directions aloud. Put a ✔ in each box to easily track the child's progress.

❑ If you wash your hair with lemonade, glue the balloon over the car.
 If you wash your hair with shampoo, glue the balloon over the audience.

❑ If a bird can fly, glue the tightrope walker on the tightrope. If a bird can't fly, glue the tightrope walker on the ground.

❑ If a shoe goes on your hand, glue the clown near the audience. If a shoe goes on your foot, glue the clown near the car.

❑ If you go to sleep when you are tired, glue the lion in the ring. If you don't go to sleep when you are tired, glue the lion by the audience.

❑ If a ball is bigger than an ant, glue the elephant near the lion. If an ant is bigger than a ball, glue the elephant away from the lion.

❑ If a square has three sides, glue the ball near the ring. If a square has four sides, glue the ball near the audience.

Additional Activities:

1. Describe a clown.

2. What is your favorite color balloon?

3. What does a tightrope walker do?

4. What kinds of animals are in a circus?

5. Have you ever been to the circus?

Give a copy of the pictures below to the child.

Conditional Directions

#BK-307 Say & Glue® for Language & Listening Fun Sheets • ©2003 Super Duper® Publications • www.superduperinc.com • 1-800-277-8737

Circus

Directions: Color and cut out all of the pictures on page 56. Follow the directions to glue those pictures on this picture scene.

Name _____

Date _____

Homework Partner _____

Camp-Out

Directions: Give the child a copy of the picture scene on page 59, and the pictures below. Have the child color and cut out all of the pictures.

Activity: Ask the child to listen carefully. Read the following directions aloud. Put a ✔ in each box to easily track the child's progress.

❏ If a brick is heavy, glue the chair beside the fire. If a brick is light, glue the chair beside the tree.

❏ If you can play soccer without a ball, glue the lantern under the tree. If you need a ball to play soccer, glue the lantern on the table.

❏ If a shoe has shoelaces, glue the bicycle beside the tree. If a shoe has buttons, glue the bicycle beside the tent.

❏ If a dog wears pajamas, glue the fishing pole beside the tent. If a dog wears a collar, glue the fishing pole beside the table.

❏ If a fireman puts out fires, glue the radio on the table. If a pilot puts out fires, glue the radio beside the fire.

❏ If Friday comes after Wednesday, glue the sleeping bag by the tent. If Wednesday comes after Friday, glue the sleeping bag under the tree.

Additional Activities:

1. What do you sleep in when you're camping?

2. Do you build a campfire inside a house?

3. Tell how to make a campfire.

4. What is a tent used for?

5. Name something you can roast over a fire.

Give a copy of the pictures below to the child.

Conditional Directions

#BK-307 Say & Glue® for Language & Listening Fun Sheets • ©2003 Super Duper® Publications • www.superduperinc.com • 1-800-277-8737

Camp-Out

Directions: Color and cut out all of the pictures on page 58. Follow the directions to glue those pictures on this picture scene.

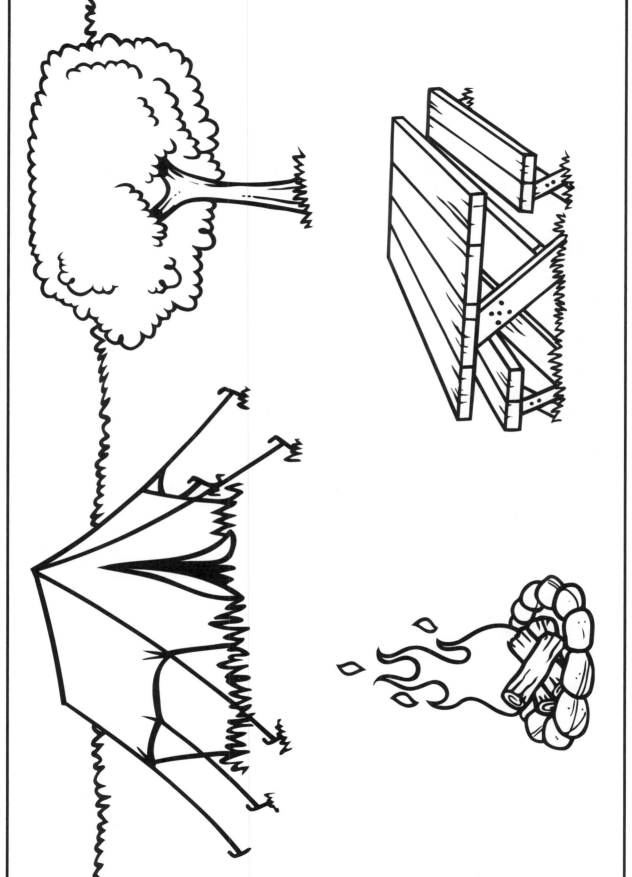

Homework Partner _____ Date _____ Name _____

Conditional Directions

#BK-307 Say & Glue® for Language & Listening Fun Sheets • ©2003 Super Duper® Publications • www.superduperinc.com • 1-800-277-8737

Lake Trip

Directions: Give the child a copy of the picture scene on page 61, and the pictures below. Have the child color and cut out all of the pictures.

Activity: Ask the child to listen carefully. Read the following directions aloud. Put a ✔ in each box to easily track the child's progress.

❏ If you can cut an apple, glue the canoe in the water. If you can't cut an apple, glue the canoe on the dock.

❏ If an orange is a fruit, glue the dog near the cabin. If an orange is a vegetable, glue the dog near the tree.

❏ If you tell time with a rug, glue the bicycle near the dock. If you tell time with a clock, glue the bicycle near the tree.

❏ If the sun makes you hot, glue the fish near the canoe. If the sun makes you cold, glue the fish near the dock.

❏ If you watch a radio, glue the life jacket near the cabin. If you listen to a radio, glue the life jacket on the dock.

❏ If a yo-yo is a toy, glue the truck near the cabin. If a yo-yo isn't a toy, glue the truck near the tree.

Additional Activities:

1. Can you swim in a lake?

2. What can you do on a dock?

3. How are a lake and the ocean alike?

4. Name somewhere else you can swim.

5. Tell about a time you went swimming.

Give a copy of the pictures below to the child.

Conditional Directions

#BK-307 Say & Glue® for Language & Listening Fun Sheets • ©2003 Super Duper® Publications • www.superduperinc.com • 1-800-277-8737

Lake Trip

Directions: Color and cut out all of the pictures on page 60. Follow the directions to glue those pictures on this picture scene.

Name

Date

Homework Partner

Playground

Directions: Give the child a copy of the picture scene on page 63, and the pictures below. Have the child color and cut out all of the pictures.

Activity: Ask the child to listen carefully. Read the following directions aloud. Put a ✔ in each box to easily track the child's progress.

❏ If you sweep with a mop, glue the sandbox near the slide. If you sweep with a broom, glue the sandbox near the bench.

❏ If you use a calculator to do math, glue the basketball near the bench. If you use a microscope to do math, glue the basketball near the slide.

❏ If three is a number, glue the see-saw near the tree. If three is a letter, glue the see-saw near the slide.

❏ If an apple grows on the ground, glue the boy near the slide. If an apple grows on a tree, glue the boy near the swings.

❏ If a bear lives in a cave, glue the flowers under the tree. If a bear lives in the water, glue the flowers beside the bench.

❏ If you push a bike, glue the monkey bars near the tree. If you pedal a bike, glue the monkey bars near the swings.

Additional Activities:

1. Tell about a time you went to a playground.

2. Name two things you find at a playground.

3. What can you do in a sandbox?

4. Can you climb at a playground? If so, what can you climb on?

5. What is your favorite thing to do at a playground?

Give a copy of the pictures below to the child.

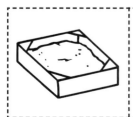     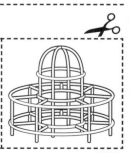

#BK-307 Say & Glue® for Language & Listening Fun Sheets • ©2003 Super Duper® Publications • www.superduperinc.com • 1-800-277-8737

Playground

Directions: Color and cut out all of the pictures on page 62. Follow the directions to glue those pictures on this picture scene.

Name _____

Date _____

Homework Partner _____

Tommy's Good Day

Directions: Give the child a copy of the picture scene on page 65, and the pictures below. Have the child color and cut out all of the pictures.

Activity: Ask the child to listen carefully. Read the story aloud. After listening to the story, have the child glue the pictures on the page according to the details in the story.

Tommy knew it was going to be a great day right from the beginning. He woke up nice and warm because his favorite blanket had stayed on his bed all night. His new pillow had stayed under his head all night as well and had helped him get a good night's sleep. He decided to wear his favorite hat and found it on the top shelf of his closet. His new shoes were beside his bed just waiting for him to put them on. Tommy heard his Mom call him. He knew she was cooking his favorite breakfast of pancakes and bacon today. It was going to be a great day!

Additional Activities:

1. Where was Tommy?

2. What time of day was it in the story?

3. What did Tommy have new on his bed?

4. Who called Tommy?

5. What was Mom cooking?

Give a copy of the pictures below to the child.

 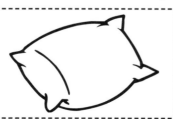 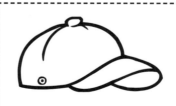 

Semantic Recall

#BK-307 Say & Glue® for Language & Listening Fun Sheets • ©2003 Super Duper® Publications • www.superduperinc.com • 1-800-277-8737

Tommy's Good Day

Directions: Color and cut out all of the pictures on page 64. Glue the pictures on the scene according to the details in the story.

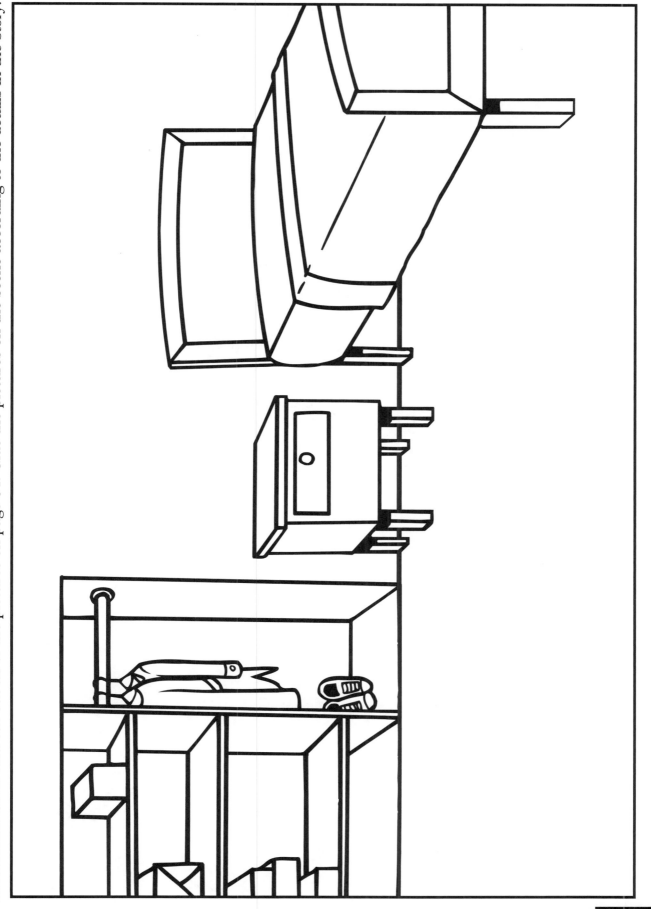

Name

Date

Homework Partner

Time for Supper

Directions: Give the child a copy of the picture scene on page 67, and the pictures below. Have the child color and cut out all of the pictures.

Activity: Ask the child to listen carefully. Read the story aloud. After listening to the story, have the child glue the pictures on the page according to the details in the story.

Gracie ate an early lunch today, and was ready for supper. She was so hungry! When she went into the kitchen, she looked at the clock over the refrigerator and saw that it was close to supper time. She didn't see Mom, but she saw a pot on the stove and the silverware on the counter. Gracie knew that supper must almost be ready. She decided to get a drink until it was time to eat. She looked around and found the pitcher on the table. She poured herself a drink and sat down to wait for Mom. Gracie hoped that they would eat soon!

Additional Activities:

1. What was wrong with Gracie?

2. What did Gracie want to do?

3. Was Gracie's mom with her?

4. What did Gracie see on the stove?

5. Where was the pitcher?

Give a copy of the pictures below to the child.

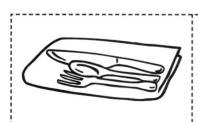   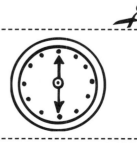

Semantic Recall

#BK-307 Say & Glue® for Language & Listening Fun Sheets · ©2003 Super Duper® Publications · www.superduperinc.com · 1-800-277-8737

Time for Supper

Directions: Color and cut out all of the pictures on page 66. Glue the pictures on the scene according to the details in the story.

Homework Partner   Date   Name

The Birthday Party

Directions: Give the child a copy of the picture scene on page 69, and the pictures below. Have the child color and cut out all of the pictures.

Activity: Ask the child to listen carefully. Read the story aloud. After listening to the story, have the child glue the pictures on the page according to the details in the story.

Lindsey was so excited. It was her best friend Brandon's birthday, and she was going to his party. She went to his house early to help set up, and Brandon's dad gave her a hat to put on. Brandon didn't have his hat on yet. She put her present on the long table and went to look at the cake, which was on the round table. Brandon's mom was ready to hang the birthday banner. Brandon and Lindsey helped her hang it on the big window. This party was going to be fun!

Additional Activities:

1. Where was Lindsey going?

2. What did Brandon's dad give Lindsey to wear?

3. Where did she put her present?

4. What did Lindsey and Brandon help hang?

5. Where did they hang it?

Give a copy of the pictures below to the child.

Semantic Recall

#BK-307 Say & Glue® for Language & Listening Fun Sheets   ©2003 Super Duper® Publications   •   www.superduperinc.com   •   1-800-277-8737

The Birthday Party

Directions: Color and cut out all of the pictures on page 68. Glue the pictures on the scene according to the details in the story.

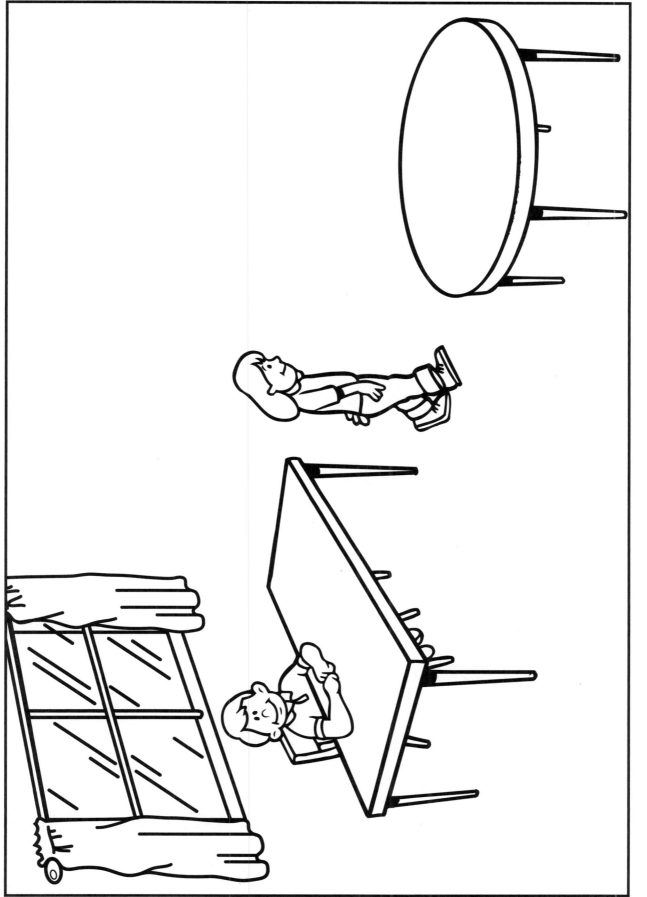

Name _____

Date _____

Homework Partner _____

A Day at the Fair

Directions: Give the child a copy of the picture scene on page 71, and the pictures below. Have the child color and cut out all of the pictures.

Activity: Ask the child to listen carefully. Read the story aloud. After listening to the story, have the child glue the pictures on the page according to the details in the story.

It was time for the fair to come into town, and Josh was meeting his friend Andrew there. Josh decided he would buy his tickets before he met Andrew. He found the ticket booth beside the gate and bought $5.00 worth of tickets. There was a clown beside the swings selling balloons. Josh bought one, but let go of it and it floated over the merry-go-round. Finally, he saw Andrew standing beside the Ferris wheel. Andrew was wearing his favorite hat. Josh ran to meet Andrew. They were going to have a great time!

Additional Activities:

1. Who was Josh meeting at the fair?

2. What two things did he buy before he met his friend?

3. What happened to his balloon?

4. Where did he find Andrew?

5. What was Andrew wearing?

Give a copy of the pictures below to the child.

#BK-307 Say & Glue® for Language & Listening Fun Sheets • ©2003 Super Duper® Publications • www.superduperinc.com • 1-800-277-8737

A Day at the Fair

Directions: Color and cut out all of the pictures on page 70. Glue the pictures on the scene according to the details in the story.

Semantic Recall

A New School Year

Directions: Give the child a copy of the picture scene on page 73, and the pictures below. Have the child color and cut out all of the pictures.

Activity: Ask the child to listen carefully. Read the story aloud. After listening to the story, have the child glue the pictures on the page according to the details in the story.

Mrs. Waites was excited about her new school year. She had her room all ready for her new students. The books were on the round table and the computer was on the table beside the door. She already had a bright, shiny apple on her desk. The clock beside the blackboard showed that it was almost time for the students to arrive. This was going to be a great year!

Additional Activities:

1. What was the name of the teacher in the story?

2. Where were the books?

3. What was on the table beside the door?

4. What did she have on her desk?

5. Where was her clock?

Give a copy of the pictures below to the child.

Semantic Recall

#BK-307 Say & Glue® for Language & Listening Fun Sheets · ©2003 Super Duper® Publications · www.superduperinc.com · 1-800-277-8737

A New School Year

Directions: Color and cut out all of the pictures on page 72. Glue the pictures on the scene according to the details in the story.

Reading
pages 4-9
Math
pages 9-12

Homework Partner ____________ Date ________ Name ____________

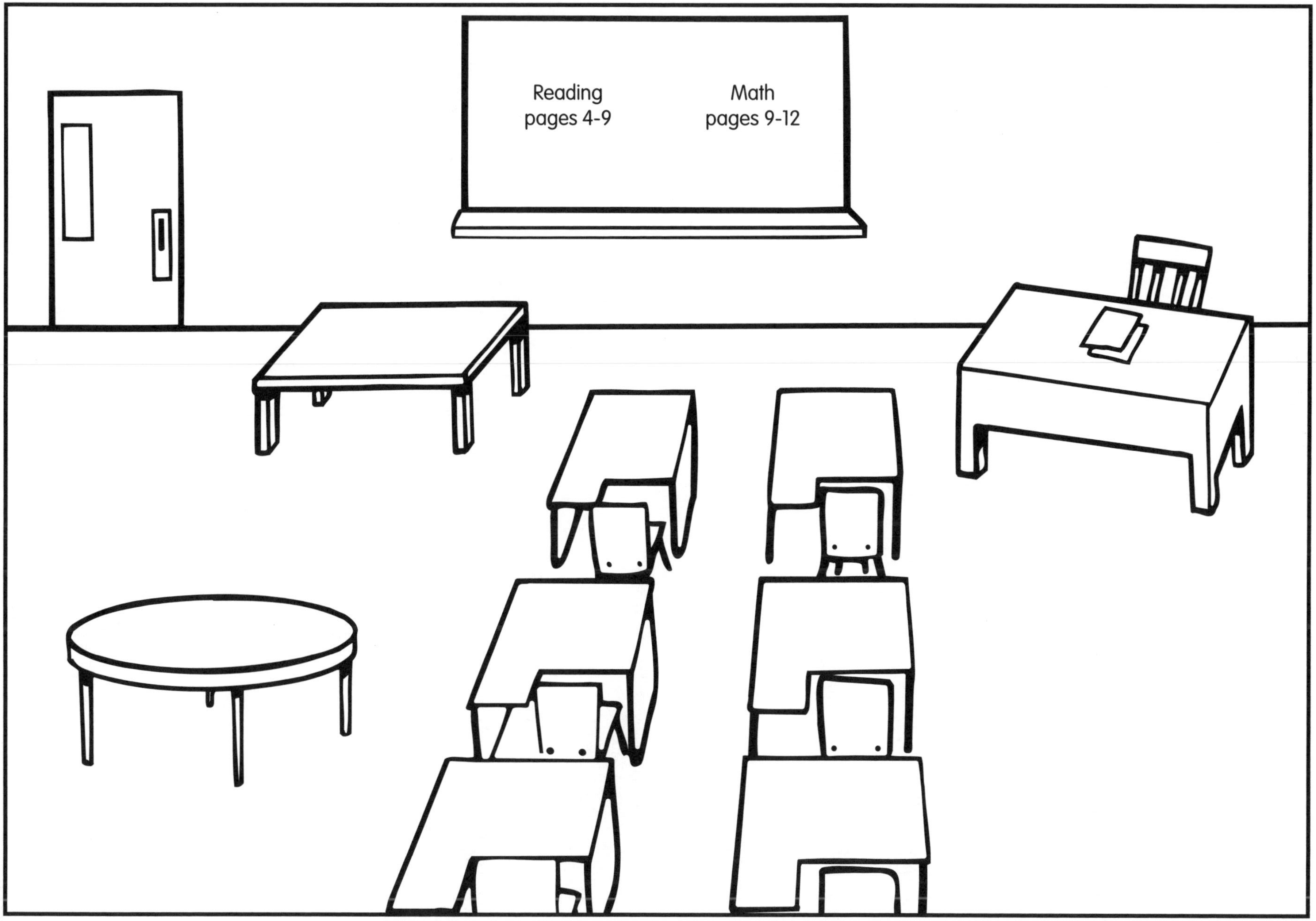

The Picnic

Directions: Give the child a copy of the picture scene on page 75, and the pictures below. Have the child color and cut out all of the pictures.

Activity: Ask the child to listen carefully. Read the story aloud. After listening to the story, have the child glue the pictures on the page according to the details in the story.

The Matthews family was going on a picnic. They drove around until they found the perfect spot with a table close by. Mrs. Matthews put the basket on the table while the boys went to play ball. At first they couldn't find the bat, but they finally found it under a tree. They heard something in the tree and looked up to see a bird watching them. Mr. Matthews was hungry so he fixed his plate and put it on the blanket. It was a great day for a picnic!

Additional Activities:

1. Where was the Matthews family going?

2. Where did Mrs. Matthews put the basket?

3. What did the boys play?

4. Where was the bat?

5. What did they hear in the tree?

Give a copy of the pictures below to the child.

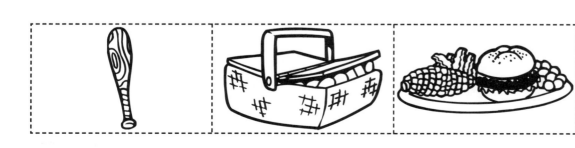

Semantic
Recall

#BK-307 Say & Glue® for Language & Listening Fun Sheets • ©2003 Super Duper® Publications • www.superduperinc.com • 1-800-277-8737

The Picnic

Directions: Color and cut out all of the pictures on page 74. Glue the pictures on the scene according to the details in the story.

The Beach Trip

Directions: Give the child a copy of the picture scene on page 77, and the pictures below. Have the child color and cut out all of the pictures.

Activity: Ask the child to listen carefully. Read the story aloud. After listening to the story, have the child glue the pictures on the page according to the details in the story.

Katie and her family had finally made it to the beach! She couldn't decide what to do first because she was so excited. She put her shoes beside the umbrella and went to build a sandcastle. She laughed at the seagull walking across the blanket. When her castle was finished, she left her sand toys beside the blanket and went to find her mom. She saw her mom's chair under the umbrella, but it was empty. Then, she heard Mom calling her. She was out swimming in the ocean. Katie ran out to the water to swim with her. The beach was so much fun!

Additional Activities:

1. Where was Katie and her family?

2. What did Katie do first at the beach?

3. What was walking across their blanket?

4. Did Katie find Mom in her chair?

5. Who did Katie swim with?

Give a copy of the pictures below to the child.

Semantic Recall

#BK-307 Say & Glue® for Language & Listening Fun Sheets • ©2003 Super Duper® Publications • www.superduperinc.com • 1-800-277-8737

The Beach Trip

Directions: Color and cut out all of the pictures on page 76. Glue the pictures on the scene according to the details in the story.

Homework Partner   Date   Name

Extension Activities for Auditory Processing

Extension activities give the therapist/teacher and parent an opportunity to reinforce the target skills at home and school.

1. Name multi-step directions for child to follow (e.g., touch your nose and clap your hands). Increase difficulty level by adding more steps.

2. Play "Grandmother's Trunk" game. Player 1 names an object (any category). Player 2 must name player 1's item, and then add one of his own. Player 3 must name first two items before adding another. Play continues until everyone has had a turn, with each player naming all objects said previously before adding one. Player 1 then names all objects before adding a new one. See how many times you can go around before someone forgets an item.

3. Read a short story. Ask the child details about the story. Also see if the child can re-tell the story to you.

4. Give the child a word to remember. Wait two minutes and see if they can recall the word. Increase difficulty by adding more words and a longer time frame.

5. Before reading a short story, give the child a category to listen for (e.g., people's names). After the story, have the child tell you the words they heard in the story in that category (e.g., John, Sid).

#BK-307 Say & Glue® for Language & Listening Fun Sheets • ©2003 Super Duper® Publications • www.superduperinc.com • 1-800-277-8737

A Spring Day!

Directions: Give the child a copy of the picture scene on page 81, and the pictures below. Have the child color and cut out all of the pictures.

Activity: Ask the child to listen carefully. Read the following directions aloud. Put a ✔ in each box to easily track the child's progress.

❑ Find the flowers. Glue the bee <u>on</u> one of them.

❑ A pretty butterfly! Glue it <u>on</u> the grass.

❑ A duck is ready to swim. Glue it <u>on</u> the water.

❑ The turtle wants some sun. Glue it <u>on</u> the rock.

❑ Find the ladybug. Glue it anywhere <u>on</u> the ground.

❑ I hear a bird! Glue the bird <u>on</u> the tree.

Additional Activities:

1. Describe a bee.

2. Which is bigger, a bee or a duck?

3. Name something a bird does.

4. What color is grass?

5. Describe a turtle.

Give a copy of the pictures below to the child.

Concepts: On

#BK-307 Say & Glue® for Language & Listening Fun Sheets • ©2003 Super Duper® Publications • www.superduperinc.com • 1-800-277-8737

A Spring Day!

Directions: Color and cut out all of the pictures on page 80. Follow the directions to glue those pictures on this picture scene.

Homework Partner   Date   Name

Hats On

Directions: Give the child a copy of the picture scene on page 83, and the pictures below. Have the child color and cut out all of the pictures.

Activity: Ask the child to listen carefully. Read the following directions aloud. Put a ✔ in each box to easily track the child's progress.

❏ Time to play ball! Glue the baseball hat <u>on</u> the baseball player.

❏ Yippee Yi Oh! Glue the cowboy hat <u>on</u> the cowboy.

❏ Let's go snow skiing. Glue the winter hat <u>on</u> the skier.

❏ Dress up time! Glue the sunhat <u>on</u> the girl wearing a skirt.

❏ I love football! Glue the helmet <u>on</u> the football player.

❏ A police officer has a busy job. Glue the police hat <u>on</u> the officer.

Additional Activities:

1. What does a cowboy ride?

2. Name something a baseball player uses.

3. Describe a hat you have.

4. Where do you wear a hat?

5. What does a football player wear on his head?

Give a copy of the pictures below to the child.

Concepts: On

#BK-307 Say & Glue® for Language & Listening Fun Sheets • ©2003 Super Duper® Publications • www.superduperinc.com • 1-800-277-8737

Hats On

Directions: Color and cut out all of the pictures on page 82. Follow the directions to glue those pictures on this picture scene.

Concepts:
On

Clean Up

Directions: Give the child a copy of the picture scene on page 85, and the pictures below. Have the child color and cut out all of the pictures.

Activity: Ask the child to listen carefully. Read the following directions aloud. Put a ✔ in each box to easily track the child's progress.

❏ That bed is not neat! Glue the pillow <u>off</u> of the bed.

❏ The covers are messy, too! Glue the covers <u>off</u> of the bed.

❏ Someone didn't put up the book. Glue it <u>off</u> of the shelf.

❏ The toys are also messy. Glue the boat <u>off</u> of the shelf.

❏ The schoolwork is not finished! Glue the papers <u>off</u> of the desk.

❏ Oh no! The lamp fell over. Glue the lamp <u>off</u> of the nightstand.

Additional Activities:

1. Describe your room.

2. Name something you can sleep on.

3. Name something on a bed.

4. What do you use a blanket for?

5. Is a pillow soft or hard?

Give a copy of the pictures below to the child.

Concepts: Off

#BK-307 Say & Glue® for Language & Listening Fun Sheets · ©2003 Super Duper® Publications · www.superduperinc.com · 1-800-277-8737

Clean Up

Directions: Color and cut out all of the pictures on page 84. Follow the directions to glue those pictures on this picture scene.

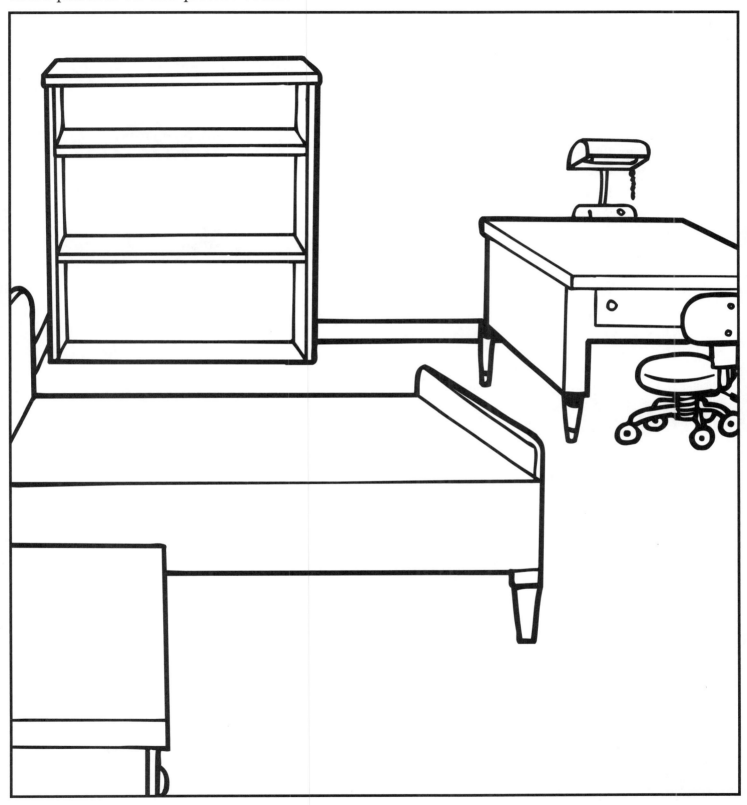

Homework Partner   Date   Name

Junk Yard

Directions: Give the child a copy of the picture scene on page 87, and the pictures below. Have the child color and cut out all of the pictures.

Activity: Ask the child to listen carefully. Read the following directions aloud. Put a ✔ in each box to easily track the child's progress.

❏ Oh no, we lost the tire! Glue it <u>off</u> of the car.

❏ The door is also missing. Glue it <u>off</u> of the car.

❏ Where did the hood go? Glue it <u>off</u> of the car.

❏ The light just fell off! Glue it <u>off</u> of the car.

❏ The antenna broke! Glue it <u>off</u> of the car.

❏ There goes the bumper! Glue it <u>off</u> of the car.

Additional Activities:

1. What is the shape of a tire?

2. Why do you need a door on a car?

3. What does a light do?

4. What makes a car go?

5. Why does a car need gas?

Give a copy of the pictures below to the child.

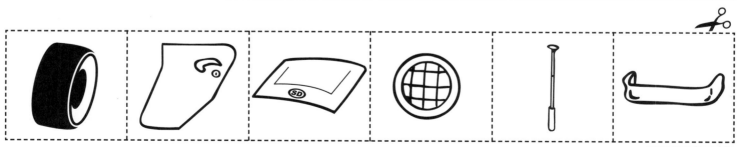

Concepts: Off

#BK-307 Say & Glue® for Language & Listening Fun Sheets · ©2003 Super Duper® Publications · www.superduperinc.com · 1-800-277-8737

Junk Yard

Directions: Color and cut out all of the pictures on page 86. Follow the directions to glue those pictures on this picture scene.

Homework Partner   Date   Name

x

x

x

**Concepts:
Off**

x

A Mountain View

Directions: Give the child a copy of the picture scene on page 89, and the pictures below. Have the child color and cut out all of the pictures.

Activity: Ask the child to listen carefully. Read the following directions aloud. Put a ✔ in each box to easily track the child's progress.

❏ The snake is swimming in the stream. Glue him at the <u>bottom</u> of the waterfall.

❏ A fish needs water! Glue the fish at the <u>bottom</u> of the waterfall.

❏ A big rock came loose! Glue the rock at the <u>bottom</u> of the mountain.

❏ I love flowers! Glue the flower at the <u>bottom</u> of the mountain.

❏ The rabbit is looking for some shade. Glue him at the <u>bottom</u> of a tree.

❏ An apple fell off! Glue it at the <u>bottom</u> of a tree.

Additional Activities:

1. How are a beach and a mountain different?

2. Name something that grows outside.

3. Name a color of a flower.

4. Describe a rock.

5. What can you do in a mountain stream?

 Give a copy of the pictures below to the child.

Concepts: Bottom

#BK-307 Say & Glue® for Language & Listening Fun Sheets · ©2003 Super Duper® Publications · www.superduperinc.com · 1-800-277-8737

A Mountain View

Directions: Color and cut out all of the pictures on page 88. Follow the directions to glue those pictures on this picture scene.

Homework Partner

Date

Name

#BK-307 Say & Glue® for Language & Listening Fun Sheets • ©2003 Super Duper® Publications • www.superduperinc.com • 1-800-277-8737

Concepts:
Bottom

89

Time to Move

Directions: Give the child a copy of the picture scene on page 91, and the pictures below. Have the child color and cut out all of the pictures.

Activity: Ask the child to listen carefully. Read the following directions aloud. Put a ✔ in each box to easily track the child's progress.

❑ This box is heavy! Glue it on the <u>bottom</u> of the stack of boxes.

❑ Be careful with the dishes! Glue the dishes at the <u>bottom</u> of the stack of dishes.

❑ Don't forget the games. Glue the game at the <u>bottom</u> of the stack of games.

❑ We like to read. Glue the book at the <u>bottom</u> of the stack of books.

❑ We have lots of clothes. Glue the shirt at the <u>bottom</u> of the stack of clothes.

❑ Shoes are everywhere! Glue the shoe at the <u>bottom</u> of the pile of shoes.

Additional Activities:

1. What can you do with a box?

2. What is a plate used for?

3. Name something you can keep on a bookshelf.

4. Name a shape a box can be.

5. What do you do with a game?

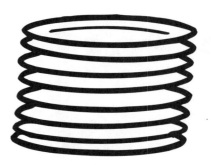

Give a copy of the pictures below to the child.

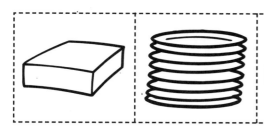   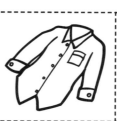 

Concepts: Bottom

#BK-307 Say & Glue® for Language & Listening Fun Sheets • ©2003 Super Duper® Publications • www.superduperinc.com • 1-800-277-8737

Time to Move

Directions: Color and cut out all of the pictures on page 90. Follow the directions to glue those pictures on this picture scene.

We All Scream for Ice Cream!

Directions: Give the child a copy of the picture scene on page 93, and the pictures below. Have the child color and cut out all of the pictures.

Activity: Ask the child to listen carefully. Read the following directions aloud. Put a ✔ in each box to easily track the child's progress.

❏ I love a banana split! Glue 3 scoops of ice cream <u>on top</u> of the banana.

❏ Glue the whip cream <u>on top</u> of the ice cream on the banana split.

❏ Glue 2 cherries <u>on top</u> of the whip cream.

❏ Glue 1 cherry <u>on top</u> of the sundae.

❏ I want more ice cream! Glue 2 scoops of ice cream <u>on top</u> of the ice cream in the bowl.

❏ I love chocolate sprinkles. Glue the sprinkles <u>on top</u> of each dessert.

Additional Activities:

1. Where do you keep ice cream?

2. Is ice cream hot or cold?

3. What can you put on top of ice cream?

4. What do you need to eat ice cream?

5. Name two ice cream flavors.

Give a copy of the pictures below to the child.

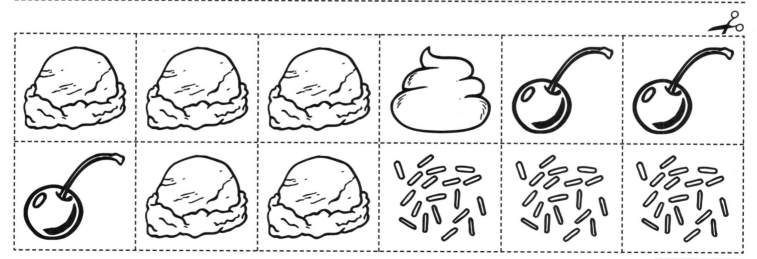

#BK-307 Say & Glue® for Language & Listening Fun Sheets • ©2003 Super Duper® Publications • www.superduperinc.com • 1-800-277-8737

We All Scream for Ice Cream!

Directions: Color and cut out all of the pictures on page 92. Follow the directions to glue those pictures on this picture scene.

Concepts: On Top

Time for Dessert

Directions: Give the child a copy of the picture scene on page 95, and the pictures below. Have the child color and cut out all of the pictures.

Activity: Ask the child to listen carefully. Read the following directions aloud. Put a ✔ in each box to easily track the child's progress.

❑ I love chocolate chip cookies! Glue one chocolate chip <u>on top</u> of each cookie.

❑ It's time for a party! Glue the candle <u>on top</u> of the cake.

❑ I love whip cream on my pudding. Glue the whip cream <u>on top</u> of each pudding.

❑ Pie tastes great with ice cream. Glue the scoop of ice cream <u>on top</u> of the pie.

❑ Cherries make it better. Glue a cherry <u>on top</u> of each pudding.

❑ Be careful not to spill your milkshake. Glue the lid <u>on top</u> of the milkshake cup.

Additional Activities:

1. How are ice cream and pudding different?

2. Is a hamburger a dessert?

3. Name your favorite dessert.

4. What do you put on top of a birthday cake?

5. Name a dessert that isn't cold.

Give a copy of the pictures below to the child.

Concepts: On Top

#BK-307 Say & Glue® for Language & Listening Fun Sheets · ©2003 Super Duper® Publications · www.superduperinc.com · 1-800-277-8737

Time for Dessert

Directions: Color and cut out all of the pictures on page 94. Follow the directions to glue those pictures on this picture scene.

Animal Homes

Directions: Give the child a copy of the picture scene on page 97, and the pictures below. Have the child color and cut out all of the pictures.

Activity: Ask the child to listen carefully. Read the following directions aloud. Put a ✔ in each box to easily track the child's progress.

❏ Glue the fish <u>inside</u> the fish bowl.

❏ Glue the dog <u>inside</u> his house.

❏ Glue the bird <u>inside</u> the birdcage.

❏ Glue the cat <u>inside</u> the cat bed.

❏ Glue the gerbil <u>inside</u> his cage.

❏ Glue the turtle <u>inside</u> the aquarium.

Additional Activities:

1. What lives in the water?

2. How are a cat and a dog different?

3. Does a bird have fur or feathers?

4. Name an animal that has fur.

5. Where can a bird live?

Give a copy of the pictures below to the child.

Concepts: Inside

#BK-307 Say & Glue® for Language & Listening Fun Sheets • ©2003 Super Duper® Publications • www.superduperinc.com • 1-800-277-8737

Animal Homes

Directions: Color and cut out all of the pictures on page 96. Follow the directions to glue those pictures on this picture scene.

Bowls of Food

Directions: Give the child a copy of the picture scene on page 99, and the pictures below. Have the child color and cut out all of the pictures.

Activity: Ask the child to listen carefully. Read the following directions aloud. Put a ✔ in each box to easily track the child's progress.

❑ Find the bowl of grapes. Glue the grape <u>inside</u> of it.

❑ I love meatballs! Glue the meatball <u>inside</u> the bowl of spaghetti.

❑ The rice needs some gravy. Glue the gravy <u>inside</u> the bowl of rice.

❑ Time for popcorn! Glue the popcorn <u>inside</u> the bowl of popcorn.

❑ Find the bowl of ice cream. Glue the scoop of ice cream <u>inside</u> of it.

❑ Find the bowl of chips. Glue the chip <u>inside</u> it.

Additional Activities:

1. Name a color that grapes can be.

2. Name something you can put on rice.

3. What does spaghetti look like?

4. What do you like to put on chips?

5. How do you make popcorn?

Give a copy of the pictures below to the child.

     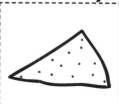

Concepts: Inside

#BK-307 Say & Glue® for Language & Listening Fun Sheets • ©2003 Super Duper® Publications • www.superduperinc.com • 1-800-277-8737

Bowls of Food

Directions: Color and cut out all of the pictures on page 98. Follow the directions to glue those pictures on this picture scene.

Homework Partner   Date   Name

Homes for All

Directions: Give the child a copy of the picture scene on page 101, and the pictures below. Have the child color and cut out all of the pictures.

Activity: Ask the child to listen carefully. Read the following directions aloud. Put a ✔ in each box to easily track the child's progress.

❏ A wolf lives in a cave. Glue the wolves <u>outside</u> of the cave.

❏ A dog lives in a doghouse. Glue the dogs <u>outside</u> of the doghouse.

❏ People live in a house. Glue the people <u>outside</u> of the house.

❏ Beavers build a home out of sticks. Glue the beavers <u>outside</u> of their dam.

❏ Birds live in a nest. Glue the birds <u>outside</u> of the nest in the tree.

❏ Snakes live in a hole. Glue the snakes <u>outside</u> of their hole.

Additional Activities:

1. Name an animal that lives in the water.

2. How are a cat and a dog alike?

3. Name an animal that lives in the woods.

4. How are a wolf and a beaver different?

5. Name an animal you could have as a pet.

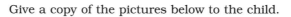
Give a copy of the pictures below to the child.

Concepts: Outside

#BK-307 Say & Glue® for Language & Listening Fun Sheets • ©2003 Super Duper® Publications • www.superduperinc.com • 1-800-277-8737

Homes for All

Directions: Color and cut out all of the pictures on page 100. Follow the directions to glue those pictures on this picture scene.

#BK-307 Say & Glue® for Language & Listening Fun Sheets • ©2003 Super Duper® Publications • www.superduperinc.com • 1-800-277-8737

Box Them Up

Directions: Give the child a copy of the picture scene on page 103, and the pictures below. Have the child color and cut out all of the pictures.

Activity: Ask the child to listen carefully. Read the following directions aloud. Put a ✔ in each box to easily track the child's progress.

❑ Someone left the marbles out. Glue the marbles <u>outside</u> of the marble box.

❑ The puzzle spilled all over. Glue the puzzle pieces <u>outside</u> of the puzzle box.

❑ The blocks are a mess! Glue the blocks <u>outside</u> of the block box.

❑ Don't step on a car! Glue the cars <u>outside</u> of the box of cars.

❑ Crayons are colorful! Glue the crayons <u>outside</u> of the box of crayons.

❑ The dolls are pretty! Glue the dolls <u>outside</u> of the box of dolls.

Additional Activities:

1. Name a food that comes in a box.

2. Tell about the toys at your house that are your favorites.

3. Name some different crayon colors.

4. Name something small you can put in a box.

5. Tell about something you can build with blocks.

- -

Give a copy of the pictures below to the child.

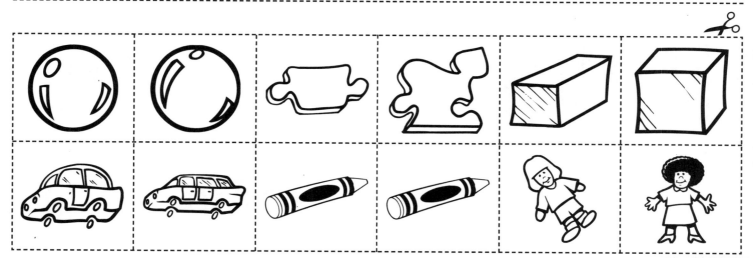

Concepts: Outside

#BK-307 Say & Glue® for Language & Listening Fun Sheets • ©2003 Super Duper® Publications • www.superduperinc.com • 1-800-277-8737

Box Them Up

Directions: Color and cut out all of the pictures on page 102. Follow the directions to glue those pictures on this picture scene.

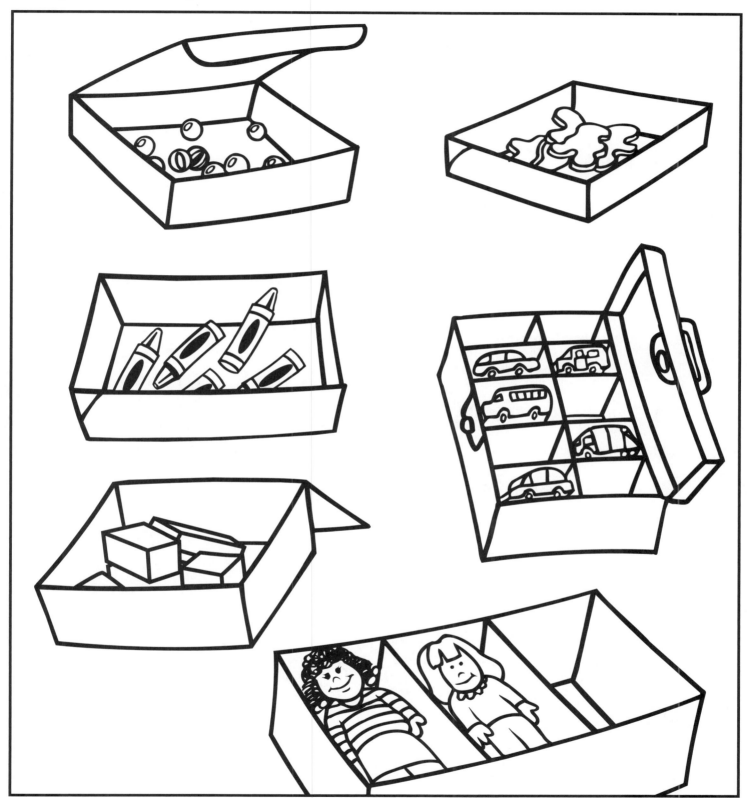

#BK-307 Say & Glue® for Language & Listening Fun Sheets • ©2003 Super Duper® Publications • www.superduperinc.com • 1-800-277-8737

Three Ring Circus

Directions: Give the child a copy of the picture scene on page 105, and the pictures below. Have the child color and cut out all of the pictures.

Activity: Ask the child to listen carefully. Read the following directions aloud. Put a ✔ in each box to easily track the child's progress.

❏ The seal is ready to play with the balls. Glue the balls <u>outside</u> of the seal ring.

❏ The clowns are so funny! Glue the clown's cars <u>outside</u> of the car ring.

❏ It's time for the dog show! Glue the dogs <u>outside</u> of the dog ring.

❏ The elephants are lost. Glue them <u>outside</u> of the seal ring.

❏ The clowns love balloons. Glue the balloons <u>outside</u> of the car ring.

❏ The dogs need some treats. Glue the dog bones <u>outside</u> of the dog ring.

Additional Activities:

1. What shape is a circus ring?

2. Tell about an act you see at the circus.

3. Name a trick a seal can do.

4. Who drives the cars at the circus?

5. What do dogs jump through?

Give a copy of the pictures below to the child.

Concepts: Outside

#BK-307 Say & Glue® for Language & Listening Fun Sheets • ©2003 Super Duper® Publications • www.superduperinc.com • 1-800-277-8737

Three Ring Circus

Directions: Color and cut out all of the pictures on page 104. Follow the directions to glue those pictures on this picture scene.

Homework Partner   Date   Name

A Sunny Day

Directions: Give the child a copy of the picture scene on page 107, and the pictures below. Have the child color and cut out all of the pictures.

Activity: Ask the child to listen carefully. Read the following directions aloud. Put a ✔ in each box to easily track the child's progress.

❏ The sun finally came out! Glue the sun so that the little cloud is <u>under</u> it.

❏ The birds are flying high! Glue them <u>under</u> the big cloud.

❏ I hear an airplane. Glue the planes <u>under</u> the birds.

❏ It's a perfect day to fly a kite. Glue the kites <u>under</u> the little cloud.

❏ What do I hear in the bushes? Glue the rabbits <u>under</u> the bushes.

❏ It's time to take a rest. Glue the girl and her book <u>under</u> the tree.

Additional Activities:

1. Does the sun make you hot or cold?

2. What do you like to do outside?

3. Where does a rabbit live?

4. How are a bird and an airplane alike?

5. What do you do with books?

Give a copy of the pictures below to the child.

Concepts: Under

#BK-307 Say & Glue® for Language & Listening Fun Sheets • ©2003 Super Duper® Publications • www.superduperinc.com • 1-800-277-8737

A Sunny Day

Directions: Color and cut out all of the pictures on page 106. Follow the directions to glue those pictures on this picture scene.

Homework Partner   Date   Name

Lots of Shelves

Directions: Give the child a copy of the picture scene on page 109, and the pictures below. Have the child color and cut out all of the pictures.

Activity: Ask the child to listen carefully. Read the following directions aloud. Put a ✔ in each box to easily track the child's progress.

❏ It's fun to read books. Glue the books on the shelf <u>under</u> the hat.

❏ Balls bounce high! Glue the balls <u>under</u> the top shelf.

❏ This doll has curly hair! Glue the dolls on the shelf <u>under</u> the balls.

❏ You can build with blocks. Glue the blocks on the shelf <u>under</u> the dolls.

❏ It's fun to race cars around the track. Glue the cars on the shelf <u>under</u> the top shelf.

❏ My favorite toy is a puzzle. Glue the puzzle on the shelf <u>under</u> the plant.

Additional Activities:

1. Name something you can keep on a shelf.

2. Tell about something on a shelf at your house.

3. Name something a shelf can be made out of.

4. What is the shape of a ball?

5. What do you do with blocks?

Give a copy of the pictures below to the child.

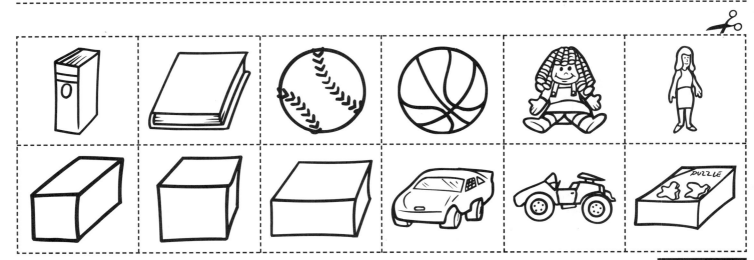

Concepts: Under

#BK-307 Say & Glue® for Language & Listening Fun Sheets • ©2003 Super Duper® Publications • www.superduperinc.com • 1-800-277-8737

Lots of Shelves

Directions: Color and cut out all of the pictures on page 108. Follow the directions to glue those pictures on this picture scene.

Homework Partner

Date

Name

Carnival Time

Directions: Give the child a copy of the picture scene on page 111, and the pictures below. Have the child color and cut out all of the pictures.

Activity: Ask the child to listen carefully. Read the following directions aloud. Put a ✔ in each box to easily track the child's progress.

- ❑ Glue two balloons <u>over</u> the roller coaster.

- ❑ Glue two balloons <u>over</u> the Carousel.

- ❑ Glue two balloons <u>over</u> the Ferris wheel.

- ❑ Glue two balloons <u>over</u> the cotton candy stand.

- ❑ Glue two balloons <u>over</u> the boy's head.

- ❑ Glue two balloons <u>over</u> the swings.

Additional Activities:

1. Name two rides at a carnival.

2. Tell about a time you went to a carnival or the fair.

3. Name two things you can eat at a carnival.

4. Does a roller coaster go fast or slow?

5. What does a balloon look like?

Give a copy of the pictures below to the child.

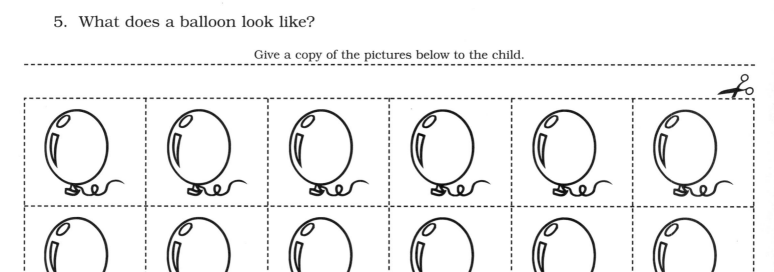

Concepts: Over

#BK-307 Say & Glue® for Language & Listening Fun Sheets • ©2003 Super Duper® Publications • www.superduperinc.com • 1-800-277-8737

Carnival Time

Directions: Color and cut out all of the pictures on page 110. Follow the directions to glue those pictures on this picture scene.

Homework Partner   Date   Name

Concepts: Over

Out in the Field

Directions: Give the child a copy of the picture scene on page 113, and the pictures below. Have the child color and cut out all of the pictures.

Activity: Ask the child to listen carefully. Read the following directions aloud. Put a ✔ in each box to easily track the child's progress.

❏ The sun is so hot! Glue the sun <u>over</u> the tree.

❏ It is starting to get cloudy. Glue the clouds <u>over</u> the barn.

❏ The birds love to fly! Glue the birds <u>over</u> the clouds.

❏ The flowers could use some rain! Glue the raindrops <u>over</u> the flowers.

❏ It's a great day to fly a kite! Glue the kites <u>over</u> the raindrops.

❏ I hear an airplane! Glue the airplane <u>over</u> the haystack.

Additional Activities:

1. Name two games you can play outside.

2. What lives in a barn?

3. Where does a bird live?

4. Name something that grows on a tree.

5. Can a dog fly a kite?

Give a copy of the pictures below to the child.

**Concepts:
Over**

#BK-307 Say & Glue® for Language & Listening Fun Sheets • ©2003 Super Duper® Publications • www.superduperinc.com • 1-800-277-8737

Out in the Field

Directions: Color and cut out all of the pictures on page 112. Follow the directions to glue those pictures on this picture scene.

Homework Partner   Date   Name

#BK-307 Say & Glue® for Language & Listening Fun Sheets • ©2003 Super Duper® Publications • www.superduperinc.com • 1-800-277-8737

In the City

Directions: Give the child a copy of the picture scene on page 115, and the pictures below. Have the child color and cut out all of the pictures.

Activity: Ask the child to listen carefully. Read the following directions aloud. Put a ✔ in each box to easily track the child's progress.

❏ We need groceries. Glue the bag <u>in front</u> of the grocery store.

❏ Someone lost his money. Glue it <u>in front</u> of the grocery store.

❏ We love to read. Glue the book <u>in front</u> of the book store.

❏ Glue the bike <u>in front</u> of the bike rack.

❏ It's time to go home. Glue the car <u>in front</u> of the toy store.

❏ Glue the truck <u>in front</u> of the stop sign.

Additional Activities:

1. Tell 2 things you can buy at the grocery store.

2. Why do you need money at a store?

3. Where can you buy books?

4. Where is a good place to keep money?

5. You can ride a bike. Name something else you can ride.

Give a copy of the pictures below to the child.

Concepts: In Front

 #BK-307 Say & Glue® for Language & Listening Fun Sheets • ©2003 Super Duper® Publications • www.superduperinc.com • 1-800-277-8737

In the City

Directions: Color and cut out all of the pictures on page 114. Follow the directions to glue those pictures on this picture scene.

Concepts: In Front

Feeding Time

Directions: Give the child a copy of the picture scene on page 117, and the pictures below. Have the child color and cut out all of the pictures.

Activity: Ask the child to listen carefully. Read the following directions aloud. Put a ✔ in each box to easily track the child's progress.

❏ The bird loves birdseed. Glue the seeds <u>in front</u> of the bird.

❏ Hay is for the elephants. Glue the hay <u>in front</u> of the elephant.

❏ The seal loves fish. Glue the fish <u>in front</u> of the seal.

❏ The lion loves a big piece of meat. Glue it <u>in front</u> of the lion.

❏ Monkeys love bananas. Glue them <u>in front</u> of the monkey.

❏ A giraffe likes leaves. Glue the leaves <u>in front</u> of the giraffe.

Additional Activities:

1. Can a person eat a banana?

2. Does a dog eat fish?

3. Name something a lion eats.

4. Can a bird eat an elephant?

5. Does an elephant eat peanuts?

Give a copy of the pictures below to the child.

Concepts: In Front

#BK-307 Say & Glue® for Language & Listening Fun Sheets · ©2003 Super Duper® Publications · www.superduperinc.com · 1-800-277-8737

Feeding Time

Directions: Color and cut out all of the pictures on page 116. Follow the directions to glue those pictures on this picture scene.

#BK-307 Say & Glue® for Language & Listening Fun Sheets • ©2003 Super Duper® Publications • www.superduperinc.com • 1-800-277-8737

Say Cheese

Directions: Give the child a copy of the picture scene on page 119, and the pictures below. Have the child color and cut out all of the pictures.

Activity: Ask the child to listen carefully. Read the following directions aloud. Put a ✔ in each box to easily track the child's progress.

❏ One child does not want to have his picture taken! Glue him <u>behind</u> the boxes.

❏ Who's next? Glue one child <u>behind</u> the chair.

❏ Be sure to wait in line. Glue one child <u>behind</u> the first person in line.

❏ Glue another child <u>behind</u> the last person in line.

❏ Glue one child <u>behind</u> the boy with the hat.

❏ The teacher is watching! Glue her <u>behind</u> the photographer.

Additional Activities:

1. What do you do with a camera?

2. What does a teacher do?

3. What do you do with film?

4. What do you like to wear to have your picture taken?

5. What do you do with a hat?

- -

Give a copy of the pictures below to the child.

#BK-307 Say & Glue® for Language & Listening Fun Sheets · ©2003 Super Duper® Publications · www.superduperinc.com · 1-800-277-8737

Say Cheese

Directions: Color and cut out all of the pictures on page 118. Follow the directions to glue those pictures on this picture scene.

#BK-307 Say & Glue® for Language & Listening Fun Sheets • ©2003 Super Duper® Publications • www.superduperinc.com • 1-800-277-8737

Repair Time

Directions: Give the child a copy of the picture scene on page 121, and the pictures below. Have the child color and cut out all of the pictures.

Activity: Ask the child to listen carefully. Read the following directions aloud. Put a ✔ in each box to easily track the child's progress.

❑ One car ran out of gas. Glue the gas pump <u>behind</u> the convertible.

❑ There are a lot of cars to work on. Glue one car <u>behind</u> the car waiting to be fixed.

❑ Glue another car <u>behind</u> the truck waiting to be fixed.

❑ A motorcycle is broken. Glue it <u>behind</u> the mechanic.

❑ We need some new tires! Glue the tires <u>behind</u> the car with no tires.

❑ Here comes another car! Glue a car <u>behind</u> the tow truck.

Additional Activities:

1. What is the difference between a car and a truck?

2. What does a tow truck do?

3. Name two things you find in a garage?

4. What is a car window made out of?

5. What do you do with a car?

Give a copy of the pictures below to the child.

Concepts: Behind

#BK-307 Say & Glue® for Language & Listening Fun Sheets • ©2003 Super Duper® Publications • www.superduperinc.com • 1-800-277-8737

Repair Time

Directions: Color and cut out all of the pictures on page 120. Follow the directions to glue those pictures on this picture scene.

Homework Partner   Date   Name

At the Dog Show

Directions: Give the child a copy of the picture scene on page 123, and the pictures below. Have the child color and cut out all of the pictures.

Activity: Ask the child to listen carefully. Read the following directions aloud. Put a ✔ in each box to easily track the child's progress.

❏ One girl is late for the show. Glue a dog <u>behind</u> her.

❏ Glue a judge <u>behind</u> the furry dog in line.

❏ Glue another dog <u>behind</u> the last dog in line.

❏ One dog ran away! Glue one dog <u>behind</u> the judges at the table.

❏ Glue a judge <u>behind</u> the first dog in line.

❏ One dog is scared. Glue a dog <u>behind</u> the boxes.

Additional Activities:

1. Tell about a pet you have.

2. Name some other animals you can have as a pet.

3. What sound does a dog make?

4. What would be a good prize at a dog show?

5. Name something a dog likes to chase.

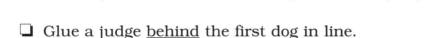

Give a copy of the pictures below to the child.

Concepts: Behind

#BK-307 Say & Glue® for Language & Listening Fun Sheets • ©2003 Super Duper® Publications • www.superduperinc.com • 1-800-277-8737

At the Dog Show

Directions: Color and cut out all of the pictures on page 122. Follow the directions to glue those pictures on this picture scene.

Homework Partner   Date   Name

#BK-307 Say & Glue® for Language & Listening Fun Sheets • ©2003 Super Duper® Publications • www.superduperinc.com • 1-800-277-8737

All Over Town

Directions: Give the child a copy of the picture scene on page 125, and the pictures below. Have the child color and cut out all of the pictures.

Activity: Ask the child to listen carefully. Read the following directions aloud. Put a ✔ in each box to easily track the child's progress.

❑ A pretty bird is flying. Glue it <u>above</u> the stop sign.

❑ It's a cloudy day. Glue the cloud <u>above</u> the house.

❑ I hear an airplane! Glue the airplane <u>above</u> the tree.

❑ Let's build a fire! Glue the smoke <u>above</u> the chimney.

❑ The sun came out! Glue it <u>above</u> the cloud.

❑ Someone is flying a kite. Glue it <u>above</u> the flowers.

Additional Activities:

1. How are a bird and an airplane alike?

2. Describe a cloud.

3. How can you make a fire?

4. What is a stop sign for?

5. Where does a bird live?

Give a copy of the pictures below to the child.

     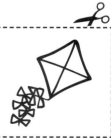

Concepts: Above

#BK-307 Say & Glue® for Language & Listening Fun Sheets • ©2003 Super Duper® Publications • www.superduperinc.com • 1-800-277-8737

All Over Town

Directions: Color and cut out all of the pictures on page 124. Follow the directions to glue those pictures on this picture scene.

#BK-307 Say & Glue® for Language & Listening Fun Sheets • ©2003 Super Duper® Publications • www.superduperinc.com • 1-800-277-8737

Time to Camp-Out

Directions: Give the child a copy of the picture scene on page 127, and the pictures below. Have the child color and cut out all of the pictures.

Activity: Ask the child to listen carefully. Read the following directions aloud. Put a ✔ in each box to easily track the child's progress.

❑ Let's build a campfire! Glue some smoke <u>above</u> the fire.

❑ Time to cook! Glue some smoke <u>above</u> the grill.

❑ The cabin has a fire inside. Glue some smoke <u>above</u> the chimney.

❑ I love roasting marshmallows! Glue some smoke <u>above</u> the marshmallows on the stick.

❑ The bats come out at night. Glue the bat <u>above</u> the tent.

❑ The moon shines brightly in the sky. Glue the moon <u>above</u> the tree.

Additional Activities:

1. Name something you take on a camping trip.

2. Name something you can roast on a fire.

3. What can you do on a camping trip?

4. Tell something that you like to do outside.

5. How are a cabin and a house alike?

Give a copy of the pictures below to the child.

✄

Concepts: Above

#BK-307 Say & Glue® for Language & Listening Fun Sheets • ©2003 Super Duper® Publications • www.superduperinc.com • 1-800-277-8737

Time to Camp-Out

Directions: Color and cut out all of the pictures on page 126. Follow the directions to glue those pictures on this picture scene.

Homework Partner   Date   Name

#BK-307 Say & Glue® for Language & Listening Fun Sheets • ©2003 Super Duper® Publications • www.superduperinc.com • 1-800-277-8737

High in the Sky

Directions: Give the child a copy of the picture scene on page 129, and the pictures below. Have the child color and cut out all of the pictures.

Activity: Ask the child to listen carefully. Read the following directions aloud. Put a ✔ in each box to easily track the child's progress.

❏ Glue a bird <u>below</u> the sun.

❏ Glue the raindrops <u>below</u> the cloud.

❏ Glue the skydiver <u>below</u> the airplane.

❏ Glue the kite <u>below</u> the bird.

❏ Glue another cloud <u>below</u> the rain.

❏ Glue another bird <u>below</u> the skydiver.

Additional Activities:

1. What do you do with a kite?

2. Tell what a cloud looks like.

3. Describe the sun.

4. Tell the difference between a bird and an airplane.

5. Who flies an airplane?

Give a copy of the pictures below to the child.

Concepts: Below

#BK-307 Say & Glue® for Language & Listening Fun Sheets • ©2003 Super Duper® Publications • www.superduperinc.com • 1-800-277-8737

High in the Sky

Directions: Color and cut out all of the pictures on page 128. Follow the directions to glue those pictures on this picture scene.

Homework Partner   Date   Name

#BK-307 Say & Glue® for Language & Listening Fun Sheets • ©2003 Super Duper® Publications • www.superduperinc.com • 1-800-277-8737

Fishy Fun!

Directions: Give the child a copy of the picture scene on page 131, and the pictures below. Have the child color and cut out all of the pictures.

Activity: Ask the child to listen carefully. Read the following directions aloud. Put a ✔ in each box to easily track the child's progress.

❏ The fish doesn't want to be caught! Glue him <u>below</u> the hook.

❏ The worm is hiding from the fish! Glue him <u>below</u> the fishing boat.

❏ A starfish is fun to look at. Glue it <u>below</u> the seaweed.

❏ Seaweed is everywhere! Glue one piece of seaweed <u>below</u> the worm.

❏ An octopus is swimming by! Glue him <u>below</u> the sailboat.

❏ Look, a treasure chest! Glue it <u>below</u> one of the fish.

Additional Activitie:

1. Where do fish live?

2. Name two things that live in the ocean.

3. What is the difference between a sailboat and a motorboat?

4. Describe an octopus.

5. What do you need to go fishing?

Give a copy of the pictures below to the child.

Concepts: Below

#BK-307 Say & Glue® for Language & Listening Fun Sheets • ©2003 Super Duper® Publications • www.superduperinc.com • 1-800-277-8737

Fishy Fun!

Directions: Color and cut out all of the pictures on page 130. Follow the directions to glue those pictures on this picture scene.

#BK-307 Say & Glue® for Language & Listening Fun Sheets • ©2003 Super Duper® Publications • www.superduperinc.com • 1-800-277-8737

In the Yard

Directions: Give the child a copy of the picture scene on page 133, and the pictures below. Have the child color and cut out all of the pictures.

Activity: Ask the child to listen carefully. Read the following directions aloud. Put a ✔ in each box to easily track the child's progress.

❏ We have a new dog. Glue him <u>near</u> the doghouse.

❏ It's time to play ball! Glue the glove <u>near</u> the bat.

❏ Let's go for a swim! Glue the float <u>near</u> the pool.

❏ The boy wants to swing. Glue him <u>near</u> the swing set.

❏ An apple fell from the tree. Glue it <u>near</u> the tree.

❏ Someone left their bike out. Glue it <u>near</u> the house.

Additional Activities:

1. What is the difference between a baseball and a basketball?

2. What do you do with a bike?

3. Name something that grows on a tree.

4. What can you do on a swing set?

5. Tell what you can do in a pool.

- Give a copy of the pictures below to the child. -

  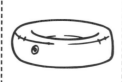   

Concepts: Near

#BK-307 Say & Glue® for Language & Listening Fun Sheets · ©2003 Super Duper® Publications · www.superduperinc.com · 1-800-277-8737

In the Yard

Directions: Color and cut out all of the pictures on page 132. Follow the directions to glue those pictures on this picture scene.

Concepts: Near

#BK-307 Say & Glue® for Language & Listening Fun Sheets • ©2003 Super Duper® Publications • www.superduperinc.com • 1-800-277-8737

At the Carnival

Directions: Give the child a copy of the picture scene on page 135, and the pictures below. Have the child color and cut out all of the pictures.

Activity: Ask the child to listen carefully. Read the following directions aloud. Put a ✔ in each box to easily track the child's progress.

❏ You need tickets to ride. Glue the ticket <u>near</u> the Ferris wheel.

❏ It's time to play a game. Glue the ball <u>near</u> the game booth.

❏ A boy wants a balloon. Glue him <u>near</u> the man selling balloons.

❏ Time to eat! Glue the cup <u>near</u> the table.

❏ I want cotton candy. Glue it <u>near</u> the cotton candy stand.

❏ A balloon got away. Glue the balloon <u>near</u> the boy.

Additional Activities:

1. Tell what you do at the fair.

2. Describe a roller coaster.

3. Name two things you see at a carnival.

4. How are a ball and a balloon different?

5. Name something you can eat at a carnival.

Give a copy of the pictures below to the child.

     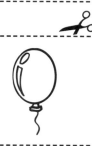

Concepts: Near

#BK-307 Say & Glue® for Language & Listening Fun Sheets • ©2003 Super Duper® Publications • www.superduperinc.com • 1-800-277-8737

At the Carnival

Directions: Color and cut out all of the pictures on page 134. Follow the directions to glue those pictures on this picture scene.

#BK-307 Say & Glue® for Language & Listening Fun Sheets • ©2003 Super Duper® Publications • www.superduperinc.com • 1-800-277-8737

Circus Time

Directions: Give the child a copy of the picture scene on page 137, and the pictures below. Have the child color and cut out all of the pictures.

Activity: Ask the child to listen carefully. Read the following directions aloud. Put a ✔ in each box to easily track the child's progress.

❏ The clowns have to be careful. Glue the car <u>far</u> from the audience.

❏ The elephant does not like the lion. Glue him <u>far</u> from the lion's cage.

❏ Don't disturb the trapeze artist! Glue the balloon <u>far</u> from the trapeze.

❏ The dogs scare the horses. Glue the dog <u>far</u> from the horse in the ring.

❏ Be careful around the car! Glue the bike <u>far</u> from the car.

❏ The clown doesn't know how to juggle. Glue him <u>far</u> from the man who is juggling balls.

Additional Activities:

1. Tell something a clown does.

2. How are a lion and a tiger different?

3. Name a trick you can do on a bike.

4. How are a horse and a dog different?

5. What does a trapeze artist do?

Give a copy of the pictures below to the child.

Concepts:
Far

#BK-307 Say & Glue® for Language & Listening Fun Sheets • ©2003 Super Duper® Publications • www.superduperinc.com • 1-800-277-8737

Circus Time

Directions: Color and cut out all of the pictures on page 136. Follow the directions to glue those pictures on this picture scene.

Homework Partner   Date   Name

Toy Time

Directions: Give the child a copy of the picture scene on page 139, and the pictures below. Have the child color and cut out all of the pictures.

Activity: Ask the child to listen carefully. Read the following directions aloud. Put a ✔ in each box to easily track the child's progress.

❑ Someone messed up the books. Glue the book <u>far</u> from the bookshelf.

❑ A game is out of place. Glue it <u>far</u> from the other games.

❑ The puzzle doesn't belong with the dolls. Glue it <u>far</u> from the dolls.

❑ Someone lost their money. Glue it <u>far</u> from the cash register.

❑ A ball is lost. Glue it <u>far</u> from the sports table.

❑ Someone moved the doll. Glue her <u>far</u> from the other dolls.

Additional Activities:

1. What do you do with a puzzle?

2. Name something you can buy in a toy store.

3. What do you do with money?

4. What do you do with a football?

5. Name three of your favorite toys.

Give a copy of the pictures below to the child.

Concepts: Far

#BK-307 Say & Glue® for Language & Listening Fun Sheets • ©2003 Super Duper® Publications • www.superduperinc.com • 1-800-277-8737

Toy Time

Directions: Color and cut out all of the pictures on page 138. Follow the directions to glue those pictures on this picture scene.

#BK-307 Say & Glue® for Language & Listening Fun Sheets • ©2003 Super Duper® Publications • www.superduperinc.com • 1-800-277-8737

Jungle Fun!

Directions: Give the child a copy of the picture scene on page 141, and the pictures below. Have the child color and cut out all of the pictures.

Activity: Ask the child to listen carefully. Read the following directions aloud. Put a ✔ in each box to easily track the child's progress.

❏ The fish don't like the snake! Glue them in the water <u>away from</u> the snake.

❏ The elephants don't like the water! Glue them <u>away from</u> the water.

❏ The men are on a safari. They are scared of what might be in the tall grass. Glue them <u>away from</u> the grass.

❏ The monkeys don't like the tiger! Glue them <u>away from</u> the tiger.

❏ The leopards want to lie in the sun and don't want any shade. Glue them <u>away from</u> the tree.

❏ The men scared the snakes away. Glue the snakes <u>away from</u> the men.

Additional Activities:

1. Name a jungle animal that is big.

2. What does a snake look like?

3. Name a jungle animal that lives in a tree.

4. What do you think it would be like to live in the jungle?

5. What do monkeys eat?

Give a copy of the pictures below to the child.

Concepts: Away From

#BK-307 Say & Glue® for Language & Listening Fun Sheets • ©2003 Super Duper® Publications • www.superduperinc.com • 1-800-277-8737

Jungle Fun!

Directions: Color and cut out all of the pictures on page 140. Follow the directions to glue those pictures on this picture scene.

Homework Partner   Date   Name

#BK-307 Say & Glue® for Language & Listening Fun Sheets • ©2003 Super Duper® Publications • www.superduperinc.com • 1-800-277-8737

Animals Galore

Directions: Give the child a copy of the picture scene on page 143, and the pictures below. Have the child color and cut out all of the pictures.

Activity: Ask the child to listen carefully. Read the following directions aloud. Put a ✔ in each box to easily track the child's progress.

❏ The ducks have lost their way! Glue them <u>away from</u> the lake.

❏ The snakes don't like the water. Glue them <u>away from</u> the lake.

❏ The butterflies like the flowers better than the trees. Glue them <u>away from</u> the tree.

❏ The turtles are tired of sunning on the rock. Glue them <u>away from</u> the rock.

❏ The dogs are afraid of the snakes. Glue them <u>away from</u> the snakes.

❏ The birds flew away from their nest. Glue them <u>away from</u> the tree.

Additional Activities:

1. How are a turtle and a snake different?

2. Where do ducks live?

3. How are a bee and a butterfly different?

4. Is a rock hard or soft?

5. Name an animal that has feathers.

Give a copy of the pictures below to the child.

Concepts: Away From

#BK-307 Say & Glue® for Language & Listening Fun Sheets • ©2003 Super Duper® Publications • www.superduperinc.com • 1-800-277-8737

Animals Galore

Directions: Color and cut out all of the pictures on page 142. Follow the directions to glue those pictures on this picture scene.

Homework Partner _____ Date _____ Name _____

#BK-307 Say & Glue® for Language & Listening Fun Sheets • ©2003 Super Duper® Publications • www.superduperinc.com • 1-800-277-8737

A Day at the Park

Directions: Give the child a copy of the picture scene on page 145, and the pictures below. Have the child color and cut out all of the pictures.

Activity: Ask the child to listen carefully. Read the following directions aloud. Put a ✔ in each box to easily track the child's progress.

❑ Nobody wants to step on the flowers! Glue them <u>away from</u> the slide.

❑ Be careful where you play ball! Glue the balls <u>away from</u> the table.

❑ These kids are finished swinging. Glue them <u>away from</u> the swing set.

❑ The sandbox is lots of fun! Glue it <u>away from</u> the monkey bars.

❑ You need lots of room to ride your bike! Glue the bike <u>away from</u> the see-saw.

❑ We love basketball! Glue the basketball <u>away from</u> the slide.

Additional Activities:

1. Name something you can do in a sandbox.

2. Tell about a park you've been to.

3. Name two things you can do at a park.

4. How are a slide and a swing different?

5. What would you do at a table in a park?

- -

Give a copy of the pictures below to the child.

Concepts: Away From

#BK-307 Say & Glue® for Language & Listening Fun Sheets • ©2003 Super Duper® Publications • www.superduperinc.com • 1-800-277-8737

A Day at the Park

Directions: Color and cut out all of the pictures on page 144. Follow the directions to glue those pictures on this picture scene.

Homework Partner   Date   Name

Back to School

Directions: Give the child a copy of the picture scene on page 147, and the pictures below. Have the child color and cut out all of the pictures.

Activity: Ask the child to listen carefully. Read the following directions aloud. Put a ✔ in each box to easily track the child's progress.

❏ The kids are ready to go home. Glue them <u>next to</u> the bus.

❏ It's time for recess! Glue the basketballs <u>next to</u> the basketball court.

❏ Somebody left their books. Glue them <u>next to</u> the school.

❏ We need some shade. Glue the tree <u>next to</u> the school.

❏ It's time for lunch! Glue the lunchbox <u>next to</u> the boy.

❏ Don't forget your bookbag! Glue the book bag <u>next to</u> one of the kids.

Additional Activities:

1. How are a bus and a car different?

2. Name two things you would find in a bookbag.

3. What do you do with a pencil?

4. Name two things you do at school.

5. Tell about your favorite part of school.

Give a copy of the pictures below to the child.

Concepts: Next To

#BK-307 Say & Glue® for Language & Listening Fun Sheets • ©2003 Super Duper® Publications • www.superduperinc.com • 1-800-277-8737

Back to School

Directions: Color and cut out all of the pictures on page 146. Follow the directions to glue those pictures on this picture scene.

Homework Partner   Date   Name

#BK-307 Say & Glue® for Language & Listening Fun Sheets • ©2003 Super Duper® Publications • www.superduperinc.com • 1-800-277-8737

Concepts:
Next To

Start Your Engines

Directions: Give the child a copy of the picture scene on page 149, and the pictures below. Have the child color and cut out all of the pictures.

Activity: Ask the child to listen carefully. Read the following directions aloud. Put a ✔ in each box to easily track the child's progress.

- ❏ A car is ready to start! Glue a car <u>next to</u> the start line.
- ❏ We need more gas! Glue the gas can <u>next to</u> the gas pump.
- ❏ We have some extra tires. Glue the tires <u>next to</u> the stack of tires.
- ❏ Uh Oh! A broken down car. Glue a car <u>next to</u> the garage.
- ❏ Another car out of gas! Glue a car <u>next to</u> the gas pump.
- ❏ We need extra tools in the shop. Glue the toolbox <u>next to</u> the garage.
- ❏ The drivers are waiting for their turn. Glue the drivers <u>next to</u> the track.
- ❏ After a hot day, a cold drink tastes great! Glue the drink machine <u>next to</u> the garage.
- ❏ One car needs new tires. Glue a car <u>next to</u> the pile of tires.
- ❏ Don't forget your helmet. Glue the helmet <u>next to</u> one of the drivers.

Additional Activities:

1. Tell why a car needs gas.
2. Describe your family's car.
3. How are a car and a motorcycle different?
4. Which is faster, a car or a tricycle?
5. Tell what you need to wash a car.

Give a copy of the pictures below to the child.

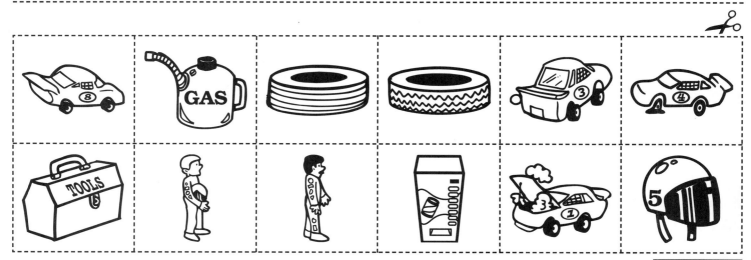

Concepts: Next To

#BK-307 Say & Glue® for Language & Listening Fun Sheets • ©2003 Super Duper® Publications • www.superduperinc.com • 1-800-277-8737

Start Your Engines

Directions: Color and cut out all of the pictures on page 148. Follow the directions to glue those pictures on this picture scene.

Homework Partner   Date   Name

#BK-307 Say & Glue® for Language & Listening Fun Sheets • ©2003 Super Duper® Publications • www.superduperinc.com • 1-800-277-8737

Time to Play

Directions: Give the child a copy of the picture scene on page 151, and the pictures below. Have the child color and cut out all of the pictures.

Activity: Ask the child to listen carefully. Read the following directions aloud. Put a ✔ in each box to easily track the child's progress.

❏ Let's play some ball! Glue the basketballs <u>next to</u> the basketball court.

❏ Two kids want to swing. Glue them <u>next to</u> the swings.

❏ One kid wants to slide. Glue one kid <u>next to</u> the slide.

❏ Two kids want to get on the merry-go-round. Glue them <u>next to</u> the merry-go-round.

❏ One kid wants to climb the tree. Glue one kid <u>next to</u> the tree.

❏ Don't forget the sand toys! Glue all the sand toys <u>next to</u> the sandbox.

Additional Activities:

1. How are baseball and basketball alike?

2. How are they different?

3. Name two sports that use a ball.

4. What do you do with a baseball bat?

5. Why does a slide have steps?

Give a copy of the pictures below to the child.

Concepts:
Next To

#BK-307 Say & Glue® for Language & Listening Fun Sheets • ©2003 Super Duper® Publications • www.superduperinc.com • 1-800-277-8737

Time to Play

Directions: Color and cut out all of the pictures on page 150. Follow the directions to glue those pictures on this picture scene.

Homework Partner   Date   Name

Concepts: Next To

A Winter Day

Directions: Give the child a copy of the picture scene on page 153, and the pictures below. Have the child color and cut out all of the pictures.

Activity: Ask the child to listen carefully. Read the following directions aloud. Put a ✔ in each box to easily track the child's progress.

❑ I want to keep my feet warm. Glue the slippers <u>beside</u> the couch.

❑ It's time to read a story. Glue the book <u>beside</u> the table.

❑ The dog likes to sleep by the fire. Glue him <u>beside</u> the fireplace.

❑ I love hot chocolate! Glue the mug <u>beside</u> the candle.

❑ I love to cuddle in a blanket. Glue the blanket <u>beside</u> the chair.

❑ We may need more wood for the fire. Glue the wood <u>beside</u> the rug.

Additional Activities:

1. What else makes your feet warm?

2. What does it look like outside during a day in the winter?

3. How do you light a candle?

4. Describe your favorite book.

5. Name two winter holidays.

Give a copy of the pictures below to the child.

Concepts: Beside

#BK-307 Say & Glue® for Language & Listening Fun Sheets • ©2003 Super Duper® Publications • www.superduperinc.com • 1-800-277-8737

A Winter Day

Directions: Color and cut out all of the pictures on page 152. Follow the directions to glue those pictures on this picture scene.

Homework Partner   Date   Name

Concepts: Beside

#BK-307 Say & Glue® for Language & Listening Fun Sheets • ©2003 Super Duper® Publications • www.superduperinc.com • 1-800-277-8737

153

A Day at School

Directions: Give the child a copy of the picture scene on page 155, and the pictures below. Have the child color and cut out all of the pictures.

Activity: Ask the child to listen carefully. Read the following directions aloud. Put a ✔ in each box to easily track the child's progress.

❏ We need to know the time. Glue the clock <u>beside</u> the board.

❏ It's time to read. Glue the book <u>beside</u> one of the desks.

❏ Someone lost a pencil. Glue it <u>beside</u> another desk.

❏ A student got in trouble. Glue the desk <u>beside</u> the teacher's desk

❏ Time to write. Glue the paper <u>beside</u> the book.

❏ Time for recess! Glue the boy <u>beside</u> the door.

Additional Activities:

1. What does a teacher do?

2. What do you do with a pencil?

3. Name something you would find in a desk.

4. What do you do with a lunchbox?

5. What do you need to draw a picture?

Give a copy of the pictures below to the child.

Concepts: Beside

#BK-307 Say & Glue® for Language & Listening Fun Sheets · ©2003 Super Duper® Publications · www.superduperinc.com · 1-800-277-8737

A Day at School

Directions: Color and cut out all of the pictures on page 154. Follow the directions to glue those pictures on this picture scene.

#BK-307 Say & Glue® for Language & Listening Fun Sheets • ©2003 Super Duper® Publications • www.superduperinc.com • 1-800-277-8737

A Day at the Beach

Directions: Give the child a copy of the picture scene on page 157, and the pictures below. Have the child color and cut out all of the pictures.

Activity: Ask the child to listen carefully. Read the following directions aloud. Put a ✔ in each box to easily track the child's progress.

❏ It's time to relax in the shade. Glue the beach chairs <u>around</u> the beach umbrella.

❏ Oh no, it's starting to get cloudy. Glue the clouds <u>around</u> the birds flying in the air.

❏ Let's play in the sand! Glue the sand toys <u>around</u> the sand castle.

❏ Time to eat! Glue the food <u>around</u> the picnic basket.

❏ The kids love to swim. Glue the kids <u>around</u> the inner tube in the water.

❏ A seagull is looking for food. Glue the breadcrumbs <u>around</u> the seagull on the beach.

Additional Activities:

1. Tell about a time you went to the beach.
2. Name something that lives in the ocean.
3. Name a game you could play on the beach.
4. What is a beach umbrella used for?
5. Name something you wear at the beach.

Give a copy of the pictures below to the child.

Concepts: Around

#BK-307 Say & Glue® for Language & Listening Fun Sheets • ©2003 Super Duper® Publications • www.superduperinc.com • 1-800-277-8737

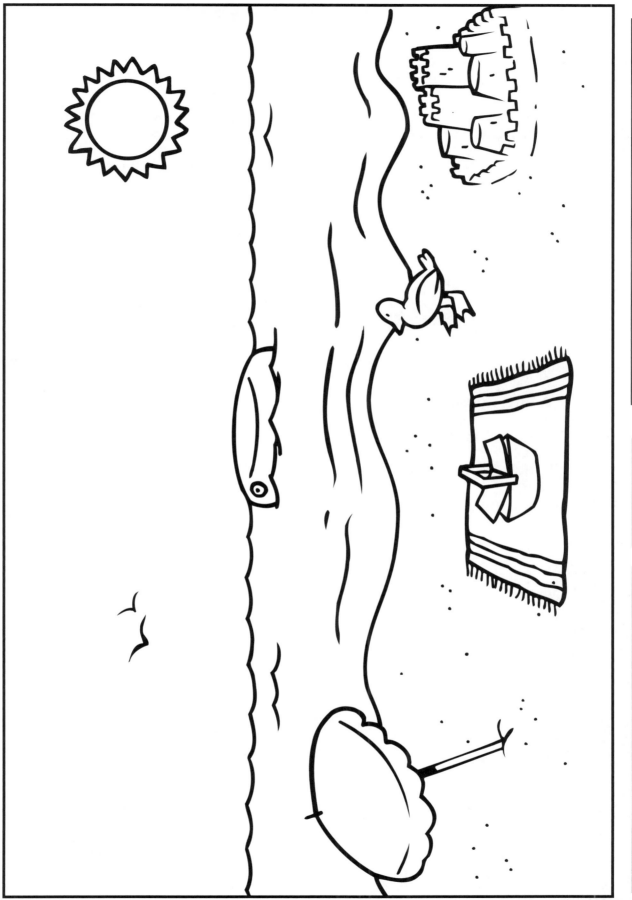

A Day at the Beach

Directions: Color and cut out all of the pictures on page 156. Follow the directions to glue those pictures on this picture scene.

Name _____

Date _____

Homework Partner _____

Out in the Yard

Directions: Give the child a copy of the picture scene on page 159, and the pictures below. Have the child color and cut out all of the pictures.

Activity: Ask the child to listen carefully. Read the following directions aloud. Put a ✔ in each box to easily track the child's progress.

❑ Let's play some ball! Glue the rest of the balls <u>around</u> the football.

❑ I love apples! Glue the rest of the apples <u>around</u> the apple on the tree.

❑ The birds are flying high! Glue the birds <u>around</u> the sun.

❑ Buzz! Buzz! Glue the bees <u>around</u> the flowers.

❑ The kids want to get wet. Glue them <u>around</u> the water sprinkler.

❑ The dogs want to rest. Glue them <u>around</u> the dog bone.

Additional Activities:

1. Name something you do in your yard.

2. Tell about a game you like to play outside.

3. Name something that grows on a tree.

Give a copy of the pictures below to the child.

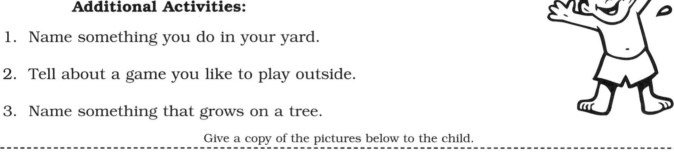

Concepts: Around

#BK-307 Say & Glue® for Language & Listening Fun Sheets • ©2003 Super Duper® Publications • www.superduperinc.com • 1-800-277-8737

Out in the Yard

Directions: Color and cut out all of the pictures on page 158. Follow the directions to glue those pictures on this picture scene.

Homework Partner Date Name

Lots of Wheels!

Directions: Give the child a copy of the picture scene on page 161, and the pictures below. Have the child color and cut out all of the pictures.

Activity: Ask the child to listen carefully. Read the following directions aloud. Put a ✔ in each box to easily track the child's progress.

❏ Let's go for a ride in the car! Glue the rest of the cars <u>around</u> the car in the picture.

❏ We need a truck for this job! Glue the rest of the trucks <u>around</u> the truck in the picture.

❏ Motorcycles are fast! Glue the rest of the motorcycles <u>around</u> the motorcycle in the picture.

❏ A bike is fun to ride! Glue the rest of the bikes <u>around</u> the bike in the picture.

❏ Someone dropped their money. Glue it <u>around</u> the drink machine.

❏ The tools didn't get put up. Glue them <u>around</u> the garage.

Additional Activities:

1. What shape is a tire?

2. Which is bigger, a bicycle wheel or a car tire?

3. Do you have a bike? If so, what color is it?

4. How many wheels are on a motorcycle?

5. How many tires are on a car?

Give a copy of the pictures below to the child.

#BK-307 Say & Glue® for Language & Listening Fun Sheets • ©2003 Super Duper® Publications • www.superduperinc.com • 1-800-277-8737

Lots of Wheels!

Directions: Color and cut out all of the pictures on page 160. Follow the directions to glue those pictures on this picture scene.

Homework Partner   Date   Name

Down on the Farm

Directions: Give the child a copy of the picture scene on page 163, and the pictures below. Have the child color and cut out all of the pictures.

Activity: Ask the child to listen carefully. Read the following directions aloud. Put a ✔ in each box to easily track the child's progress.

❑ The farmer is ready to plow the fields. Glue the tractor <u>between</u> the barns.

❑ One baby duck got lost. Glue the duck <u>between</u> the ducks on the lake.

❑ You need a pitchfork to get the hay. Glue the pitchfork <u>between</u> the haystacks.

❑ The farmer is hard at work. Glue him <u>between</u> the trees.

❑ The dog is ready for a nap. Glue him <u>between</u> the barns.

❑ The horse wants some hay to eat. Glue him <u>between</u> the haystacks.

❑ Some animals don't stay in the fence! Glue a cow <u>between</u> the fences.

❑ One cow wandered off. Glue a cow <u>between</u> the lake and the trees.

❑ The pigs are looking for their friend. Glue the pig <u>between</u> the pigs in the pen

❑ Time to feed the animals. Glue the bucket <u>between</u> the fences.

❑ The apples are falling off the tree. Glue the apples <u>between</u> the trees.

Additional Activities:

1. Name 2 games you can play outside.
2. What lives in a barn?
3. Where does a bird live?
4. Name something that grows on a tree.
5. Can a dog fly a kite?

Give a copy of the pictures below to the child.

Concepts: Between

#BK-307 Say & Glue® for Language & Listening Fun Sheets • ©2003 Super Duper® Publications • www.superduperinc.com • 1-800-277-8737

Down on the Farm

Directions: Color and cut out all of the pictures on page 162. Follow the directions to glue those pictures on this picture scene.

Homework Partner   Date   Name

#BK-307 Say & Glue® for Language & Listening Fun Sheets • ©2003 Super Duper® Publications • www.superduperinc.com • 1-800-277-8737

At the Toy Store

Directions: Give the child a copy of the picture scene on page 165, and the pictures below. Have the child color and cut out all of the pictures.

Activity: Ask the child to listen carefully. Read the following directions aloud. Put a ✔ in each box to easily track the child's progress.

❏ Time to pay for your things. Glue the money <u>between</u> the cash register and the book on the counter.

❏ Someone dropped the balls. Glue the balls <u>between</u> the other balls on the shelf.

❏ Some blocks were left out. Glue the blocks <u>between</u> the books on the top shelf.

❏ A puzzle is fun to do! Glue the puzzle on the table <u>between</u> the Jack-in-the-box and the rabbit.

❏ I love baby dolls! Glue the dolls on the shelf <u>between</u> the other dolls.

❏ Cars are so much fun to play with! Glue the cars <u>between</u> the other cars on the shelf.

Additional Activities:

1. Tell about your favorite toy.

2. What can you do with a ball?

3. How are a puzzle and a book different?

4. What do you do with a baby doll?

5. Name something you can buy at the toy store.

Give a copy of the pictures below to the child.

✂

Concepts: Between

#BK-307 Say & Glue® for Language & Listening Fun Sheets • ©2003 Super Duper® Publications • www.superduperinc.com • 1-800-277-8737

At the Toy Store

Directions: Color and cut out all of the pictures on page 164. Follow the directions to glue those pictures on this picture scene.

Homework Partner   Date   Name

On a Picnic

Directions: Give the child a copy of the picture scene on page 167, and the pictures below. Have the child color and cut out all of the pictures.

Activity: Ask the child to listen carefully. Read the following directions aloud. Put a ✔ in each box to easily track the child's progress.

❑ The ants found the food. Glue them walking <u>across</u> the blanket.

❑ Glue the boy walking <u>across</u> the bridge.

❑ I see a snake! Glue him crawling <u>across</u> the log.

❑ There are lots of bugs. Glue them walking <u>across</u> the table.

❑ Some of the ants made it to the basket. Glue them walking <u>across</u> the handle of the basket.

❑ A squirrel is looking for food. Glue him walking <u>across</u> the table.

Additional Activities

1. Name two kinds of food.

2. What do you do with a picnic basket?

3. How do you keep a drink cold?

4. How does a snake move around?

5. Name a type of bug.

- Give a copy of the pictures below to the child. -

Concepts: Across

#BK-307 Say & Glue® for Language & Listening Fun Sheets • ©2003 Super Duper® Publications • www.superduperinc.com • 1-800-277-8737

On a Picnic

Directions: Color and cut out all of the pictures on page 166. Follow the directions to glue those pictures on this picture scene.

Harbor Scene

Directions: Give the child a copy of the picture scene on page 169, and the pictures below. Have the child color and cut out all of the pictures.

Activity: Ask the child to listen carefully. Read the following directions aloud. Put a ✔ in each box to easily track the child's progress.

❏ I see a boat! Glue the boat going <u>across</u> the water.

❏ Glue the car going <u>across</u> the bridge.

❏ Our boat needs some work. Glue the man walking <u>across</u> the boat in front of the repair store.

❏ Glue the motorcycle going <u>across</u> the bridge.

❏ Someone is fixing the roof. Glue the man walking <u>across</u> the top of a building.

❏ The woman is waiting to take a ride on the boat. Glue her walking <u>across</u> the dock.

Additional Activities:

1. What do you do with a boat?

2. What do you do with a table?

3. How are a boat and an airplane different?

4. What is a bridge?

5. Why do you put a motor on a boat?

Give a copy of the pictures below to the child.

Concepts: Across

#BK-307 Say & Glue® for Language & Listening Fun Sheets • ©2003 Super Duper® Publications • www.superduperinc.com • 1-800-277-8737

Harbor Scene

Directions: Color and cut out all of the pictures on page 168. Follow the directions to glue those pictures on this picture scene.

Homework Partner   Date   Name

Concepts: Across

#BK-307 Say & Glue® for Language & Listening Fun Sheets • ©2003 Super Duper® Publications • www.superduperinc.com • 1-800-277-8737

169

Toy Time

Directions: Give the child a copy of the picture scene on page 171, and the pictures below. Have the child color and cut out all of the pictures.

Activity: Ask the child to listen carefully. Read the following directions aloud. Put a ✔ in each box to easily track the child's progress.

❏ Time for a tea party. Glue the cup to the <u>left</u> of the tea set.

❏ Let's put up the books. Glue the book to the <u>left</u> of the other books.

❏ Glue the doll to the <u>left</u> of the blocks.

❏ Glue the dump truck to the <u>left</u> of the doll.

❏ Puzzles are always fun. Glue the puzzle to the <u>left</u> of the Jack-in-the-box.

❏ I love puppets! Glue the puppet to the <u>left</u> of the cup.

Additional Activities:

1. What can you build with blocks?

2. What do some people put in their tea?

3. How do you work a puppet?

4. Describe your favorite book.

5. Where do you find shelves with toys on them?

Give a copy of the pictures below to the child.

Concepts: Left

#BK-307 Say & Glue® for Language & Listening Fun Sheets · ©2003 Super Duper® Publications · www.superduperinc.com · 1-800-277-8737

Toy Time

Directions: Color and cut out all of the pictures on page 170. Follow the directions to glue those pictures on this picture scene.

At the Car Wash

Directions: Give the child a copy of the picture scene on page 173, and the pictures below. Have the child color and cut out all of the pictures.

Activity: Ask the child to listen carefully. Read the following directions aloud. Put a ✔ in each box to easily track the child's progress.

❏ We need water to wash! Glue the bucket to the <u>left</u> of the boy.

❏ Glue the sponge to the <u>left</u> of the truck.

❏ Put some soap in the water! Glue the soap to the <u>left</u> of the bucket.

❏ Glue the brush to the <u>left</u> of the hose.

❏ We need another hose! Glue the hose to the <u>left</u> of the car.

❏ We'll need to dry everything! Glue the towel to the <u>left</u> of the soap.

Additional Activities:

1. Tell what you need to wash a car.

2. Why do you use soap to wash a car?

3. When do you wash a car?

4. Can you wash a bike?

5. What can you put in a bucket?

Give a copy of the pictures below to the child.

Concepts: Left

#BK-307 Say & Glue® for Language & Listening Fun Sheets • ©2003 Super Duper® Publications • www.superduperinc.com • 1-800-277-8737

At the Car Wash

Directions: Color and cut out all of the pictures on page 172. Follow the directions to glue those pictures on this picture scene.

**Concepts:
Left**

In the Garden

Directions: Give the child a copy of the picture scene on page 175, and the pictures below. Have the child color and cut out all of the pictures.

Activity: Ask the child to listen carefully. Read the following directions aloud. Put a ✔ in each box to easily track the child's progress.

❏ Time to plant the seeds. Glue them to the <u>right</u> of the scarecrow.

❏ The peas are starting to grow! Glue the pea to the <u>right</u> of the sign.

❏ I love corn. Glue the corn cob to the <u>right</u> of the corn plants.

❏ Time to water the flowers. Glue the watering can to the <u>right</u> of the flowers.

❏ Tomatoes are good to eat! Glue the tomato plant to the <u>right</u> of the bag of fertilizer.

❏ A big watermelon is ready to pick. Glue it to the <u>right</u> of the tomato plant.

Additional Activities:

1. Name something that grows in a garden.

2. Name two vegetables.

3. Name two fruits.

4. What do plants need to grow?

5. What color is corn?

Give a copy of the pictures below to the child.

Concepts: Right

#BK-307 Say & Glue® for Language & Listening Fun Sheets • ©2003 Super Duper® Publications • www.superduperinc.com • 1-800-277-8737

In the Garden

Directions: Color and cut out all of the pictures on page 174. Follow the directions to glue those pictures on this picture scene.

Homework Partner   Date   Name

Pizza Party

Directions: Give the child a copy of the picture scene on page 177, and the pictures below. Have the child color and cut out all of the pictures.

Activity: Ask the child to listen carefully. Read the following directions aloud. Put a ✔ in each box to easily track the child's progress.

❑ Find the pizza on the right. Glue the pepperonis on the <u>right</u> side of it.

❑ Glue the mushrooms on the <u>right</u> side of the other pizza.

❑ We need a drink. Glue the cup to the <u>right</u> of the cola bottle.

❑ Don't forget your napkin! Glue the napkin to the <u>right</u> of the plate.

❑ What about dessert? Glue the cupcake to the <u>right</u> of a pizza.

❑ I need some cheese for mine. Glue the cheese to the <u>right</u> of the napkin.

Additional Activities:

1. What shape is a pizza?

2. What can you put on a pizza?

3. Name your favorite kind of pizza.

4. Name two things you can drink.

5. Name something else you can eat.

Give a copy of the pictures below to the child.

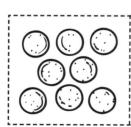     

Concepts: Right

#BK-307 Say & Glue® for Language & Listening Fun Sheets • ©2003 Super Duper® Publications • www.superduperinc.com • 1-800-277-8737

Pizza Party

Directions: Color and cut out all of the pictures on page 176. Follow the directions to glue those pictures on this picture scene.

Homework Partner   Date   Name

Concepts: Right

A Day at the Zoo

Directions: Give the child a copy of the picture scene on page 179, and the pictures below. Have the child color and cut out all of the pictures.

Activity: Ask the child to listen carefully. Read the following directions aloud. Put a ✔ in each box to easily track the child's progress.

- ❏ Find the seals on the rock. Glue the seal in the <u>middle</u> of the other seals.
- ❏ Find the snakes in the grass. Glue the snake in the <u>middle</u> of the other snakes.
- ❏ Find the fish in the pond. Glue the fish in the <u>middle</u> of the other fish.
- ❏ Find the elephants. Glue the elephant in the <u>middle</u> of the other elephants.
- ❏ The man is tired and needs a rest. Glue him in the <u>middle</u> of the bench.
- ❏ Find the giraffes. Glue the giraffe in the <u>middle</u> of the other giraffes.
- ❏ Find the zebras. Glue the zebra in the <u>middle</u> of the other zebras.
- ❏ A turtle needs some sun! Glue the turtle in the <u>middle</u> of the rock.
- ❏ We love balloons! Glue the balloon in the <u>middle</u> of the other balloons.
- ❏ Find the flower garden. Glue the flower in the <u>middle</u> of the garden.
- ❏ Find the tigers. Glue the tiger in the <u>middle</u> of the other tigers.
- ❏ Find the lions. Glue the lion in the <u>middle</u> of the other lions.

Additional Activities:

1. Name an animal that lives in the water.
2. What is the difference between a bird and a turtle?
3. Describe a snake.

Give a copy of the pictures below to the child.

Concepts: Middle

#BK-307 Say & Glue® for Language & Listening Fun Sheets • ©2003 Super Duper® Publications • www.superduperinc.com • 1-800-277-8737

A Day at the Zoo

Directions: Color and cut out all of the pictures on page 178. Follow the directions to glue those pictures on this picture scene.

Homework Partner   Date   Name

#BK-307 Say & Glue® for Language & Listening Fun Sheets • ©2003 Super Duper® Publications • www.superduperinc.com • 1-800-277-8737

Circus Fun!

Directions: Give the child a copy of the picture scene on page 181, and the pictures below. Have the child color and cut out all of the pictures.

Activity: Ask the child to listen carefully. Read the following directions aloud. Put a ✔ in each box to easily track the child's progress.

- ❏ Find the funny clown cars. Glue the car in the <u>middle</u> of the other two cars.
- ❏ Look up on the high wire! Glue the two tight-rope walkers in the <u>middle</u> of the high wire.
- ❏ We finally found a seat! Glue the two people in the <u>middle</u> of the audience.
- ❏ Wow! He can really jump! Glue the acrobat in the <u>middle</u> of the trampoline.
- ❏ It's a long way up! Glue the trapeze artist in the <u>middle</u> of the ladder.
- ❏ Look at all the dogs! Glue the dog in the <u>middle</u> of the other dogs.
- ❏ I want a balloon. Glue the balloon in the <u>middle</u> of the other balloons.
- ❏ The clowns are so funny! Glue the clown in the <u>middle</u> of the other clowns.
- ❏ It's time for the horse show. Glue the horse in the <u>middle</u> of the empty ring.
- ❏ The seals are ready to play with the balls. Glue the ball in the <u>middle</u> of the other balls.

Additional Activities:

1. How do the acrobats get up to the trapeze?

2. Name something a clown wears.

3. Where else might you see a clown?

Give a copy of the pictures below to the child.

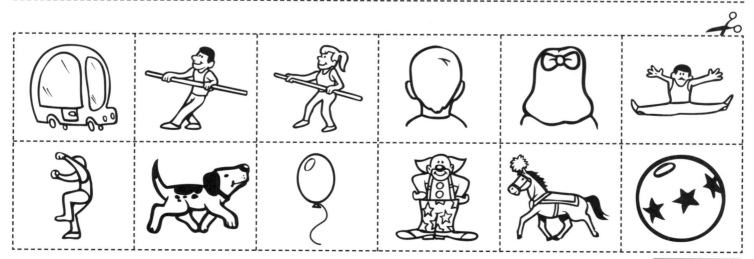

Concepts: Middle

#BK-307 Say & Glue® for Language & Listening Fun Sheets • ©2003 Super Duper® Publications • www.superduperinc.com • 1-800-277-8737

Circus Fun!

Directions: Color and cut out all of the pictures on page 180. Follow the directions to glue those pictures on this picture scene.

Homework Partner   Date   Name

Concepts: Middle

#BK-307 Say & Glue® for Language & Listening Fun Sheets · ©2003 Super Duper® Publications · www.superduperinc.com · 1-800-277-8737

In the Workshop

Directions: Give the child a copy of the picture scene on page 183, and the pictures below. Have the child color and cut out all of the pictures.

Activity: Ask the child to listen carefully. Read the following directions aloud. Put a ✔ in each box to easily track the child's progress.

❑ We're finished with the hammer. Glue the hammer in the <u>middle</u> of the other hammers.

❑ A screwdriver can be long or short. Glue the screwdriver in the <u>middle</u> of the other screwdrivers.

❑ We need to label our bench. Glue the word "tools" in the <u>middle</u> of the top piece of the bench.

❑ Time to paint! Glue the paintbrush in the <u>middle</u> of the paint can.

❑ Don't forget what's in the can. Glue the word "paint" on the <u>middle</u> of the can.

❑ Let's paint the wood. Glue the spot of paint in the <u>middle</u> of the long board.

❑ A saw is really sharp. Glue the saw so it is hanging in the <u>middle</u> of the tools.

❑ Lot's of people use a wrench. Glue the wrench in the <u>middle</u> of the other wrenches.

❑ Be careful with the pliers! Glue the pliers in the <u>middle</u> of the other pliers.

❑ It's time to nail. Glue the nail in the <u>middle</u> of the short board.

❑ Don't forget to measure. Glue the tape in the <u>middle</u> of the workbench.

❑ Always clean up your stuff. Glue the screw in the <u>middle</u> of the bucket of screws.

Additional Activities:

1. Name 2 things you could paint.
2. Tell about a time something at your house broke.
3. Name 2 tools you have at your house.

Give a copy of the pictures below to the child.

#BK-307 Say & Glue® for Language & Listening Fun Sheets • ©2003 Super Duper® Publications • www.superduperinc.com • 1-800-277-8737

Concepts: Middle

In the Workshop

Directions: Color and cut out all of the pictures on page 182. Follow the directions to glue those pictures on this picture scene.

Homework Partner   Date   Name

Concepts: Middle

#BK-307 Say & Glue® for Language & Listening Fun Sheets • ©2003 Super Duper® Publications • www.superduperinc.com • 1-800-277-8737

183

Time for Cupcakes

Directions: Give the child a copy of the picture scene on page 185, and the pictures below. Have the child color and cut out all of the pictures.

Activity: Ask the child to listen carefully. Read the following directions aloud. Put a ✔ in each box to easily track the child's progress.

❏ Cupcakes are great to eat! Glue one cupcake in each corner of the box.

For a more difficult task, follow these directions below:

❏ Glue one cupcake in the top right <u>corner</u>.

❏ Glue one cupcake in the bottom left <u>corner</u>.

❏ Glue one cupcake in the top left <u>corner</u>.

❏ Glue one cupcake in the bottom right <u>corner</u>.

Additional Activities:

1. What do you put on top of a cupcake?

2. Is a cupcake sweet or sour?

3. How are a cupcake and a cookie different?

4. What is your favorite kind of cupcake?

5. How are a cake and a cupcake alike?

Give a copy of the pictures below to the child.

Concepts: Corner

#BK-307 Say & Glue® for Language & Listening Fun Sheets • ©2003 Super Duper® Publications • www.superduperinc.com • 1-800-277-8737

Time for Cupcakes

Directions: Color and cut out all of the pictures on page 184. Follow the directions to glue those pictures on this picture scene.

Name

Date

Homework Partner

#BK-307 Say & Glue® for Language & Listening Fun Sheets • ©2003 Super Duper® Publications • www.superduperinc.com • 1-800-277-8737

At the Pool

Directions: Give the child a copy of the picture scene on page 187, and the pictures below. Have the child color and cut out all of the pictures.

Activity: Ask the child to listen carefully. Read the following directions aloud. Put a ✔ in each box to easily track the child's progress.

❑ Glue the swim ring in one <u>corner</u> of the pool.

❑ Glue the flippers in one <u>corner</u> of the pool.

❑ Glue the goggles in one <u>corner</u> of the pool

❑ Glue the raft in one <u>corner</u> of the pool.

For a more difficult task, follow these directions below:

❑ Glue the swim ring in the top right <u>corner</u> of the pool.

❑ Glue the flippers in the top left <u>corner</u> of the pool.

❑ Glue the goggles in the bottom left <u>corner</u> of the pool.

❑ Glue the raft in the bottom right <u>corner</u> of the pool.

Additional Activities:

1. What do you do with a towel?

2. Name two things you can do in a pool.

3. Name something that will float.

4. What do you do with a raft?

5. What is a mask used for?

Give a copy of the pictures below to the child.

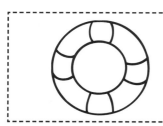   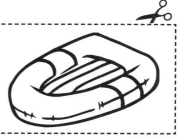

Concepts: Corner

Directions: Color and cut out all of the pictures on page 186. Follow the directions to glue those pictures on this picture scene.

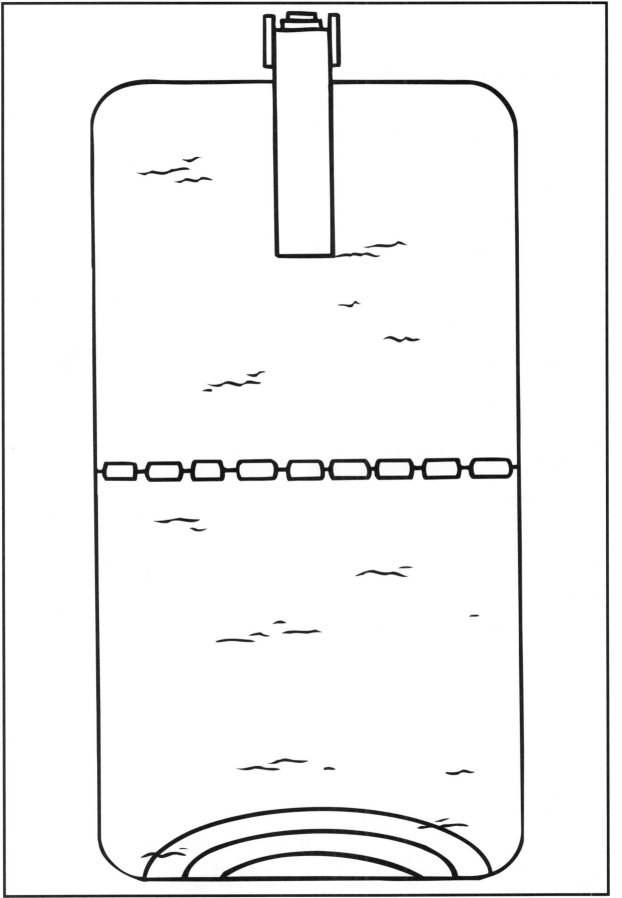

Name

Date

Homework Partner

#BK-307 Say & Glue® for Language & Listening Fun Sheets · ©2003 Super Duper® Publications · www.superduperinc.com · 1-800-277-8737

Hot Off the Grill

Directions: Give the child a copy of the picture scene on page 189, and the pictures below. Have the child color and cut out all of the pictures.

Activity: Ask the child to listen carefully. Read the following directions aloud. Put a ✔ in each box to easily track the child's progress.

- ❏ Glue the burger in one <u>corner</u> of the grill.
- ❏ Glue the hot dog in one <u>corner</u> of the grill.
- ❏ Glue the steak in one <u>corner</u> of the grill.
- ❏ Glue the chicken in one <u>corner</u> of the grill.

For a more difficult task, follow these directions below:

- ❏ Glue the burger in the top left <u>corner</u> of the grill.
- ❏ Glue the hot dog in the top right <u>corner</u> of the grill.
- ❏ Glue the steak in the bottom right <u>corner</u> of the grill.
- ❏ Glue the chicken in the bottom left <u>corner</u> of the grill.

Additional Activities:

1. What can you put on a hot dog?

2. What can you put on a hamburger?

3. Name something else you can cook on a grill.

4. How are a hot dog and a hamburger alike?

5. Is a grill hot or cold?

Give a copy of the pictures below to the child.

   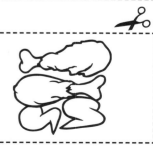

Concepts: Corner

#BK-307 Say & Glue® for Language & Listening Fun Sheets • ©2003 Super Duper® Publications • www.superduperinc.com • 1-800-277-8737

Hot Off the Grill

Directions: Color and cut out all of the pictures on page 188. Follow the directions to glue those pictures on this picture scene.

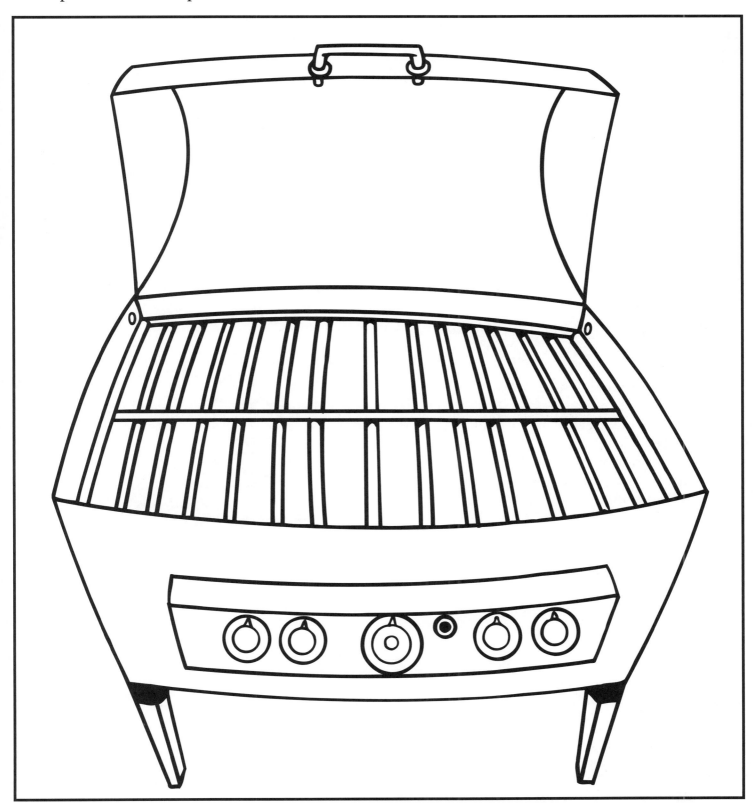

Homework Partner   Date   Name

Lots of Boxes!

Directions: Give the child a copy of the picture scene on page 191, and the pictures below. Have the child color and cut out all of the pictures.

Activity: Ask the child to listen carefully. Read the following directions aloud. Put a ✔ in each box to easily track the child's progress.

❏ Find the robot. Glue it in the <u>center</u> of the box of robots.

❏ Find the book. Glue it in the <u>center</u> of the box of books.

❏ Find the block. Glue it in the <u>center</u> of the box of blocks.

❏ Find the marble. Glue it in the <u>center</u> of the box of marbles.

❏ Find the car. Glue it in the <u>center</u> of the box of cars.

❏ Find the doll. Glue it in the <u>center</u> of the box of dolls.

Additional Activities:

1. What do you do with a book?

2. What shape is a marble?

3. What shape is a block?

4. Tell about a book you like to read.

5. Where can you play with a toy car?

Give a copy of the pictures below to the child.

**Concepts:
Center**

#BK-307 Say & Glue® for Language & Listening Fun Sheets • ©2003 Super Duper® Publications • www.superduperinc.com • 1-800-277-8737

Lots of Boxes!

Directions: Color and cut out all of the pictures on page 190. Follow the directions to glue those pictures on this picture scene.

Time to Sew

Directions: Give the child a copy of the picture scene on page 193, and the pictures below. Have the child color and cut out all of the pictures.

Activity: Ask the child to listen carefully. Read the following directions aloud. Put a ✔ in each box to easily track the child's progress.

❑ Glue one patch on the <u>center</u> of the dress.

❑ Glue one patch on the <u>center</u> of the skirt.

❑ Glue one patch on the <u>center</u> of the shirt.

❑ Glue one patch on the center of the coat.

❑ Glue one patch on the <u>center</u> of the blanket.

❑ Glue one patch on the <u>center</u> of the hat.

Additional Activities:

1. Why do you use a patch?

2. How are a skirt and dress alike?

3. What are clothes made out of?

4. Where can you buy clothes?

5. What do you do with a sewing machine?

- Give a copy of the pictures below to the child. -

✂

▢	▢	▢	▢	▢	▢

Concepts: Center

#BK-307 Say & Glue® for Language & Listening Fun Sheets • ©2003 Super Duper® Publications • www.superduperinc.com • 1-800-277-8737

Time to Sew

Directions: Color and cut out all of the pictures on page 192. Follow the directions to glue those pictures on this picture scene.

Homework Partner   Date   Name

A Messy Room

Directions: Give the child a copy of the picture scene on page 195, and the pictures below. Have the child color and cut out all of the pictures.

Activity: Ask the child to listen carefully. Read the following directions aloud. Put a ✔ in each box to easily track the child's progress.

❑ Glue the flower picture in the <u>center</u> of the frame.

❑ Glue the shoes in the <u>center</u> of the rug.

❑ Glue the shirt in the <u>center</u> of the open drawer.

❑ Glue the book in the <u>center</u> of the bed.

❑ Glue the belt in the <u>center</u> of the closet shelf.

❑ Glue the shirt so that it is hanging in the <u>center</u> of the closet.

Additional Activities:

1. Where do you put a rug?

2. Name something you can put in a drawer.

3. What do you use a closet for?

4. What is a bed for?

5. Name something you can hang in a closet.

Give a copy of the pictures below to the child.

    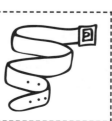 

Concepts: Center

#BK-307 Say & Glue® for Language & Listening Fun Sheets • ©2003 Super Duper® Publications • www.superduperinc.com • 1-800-277-8737

A Messy Room

Directions: Color and cut out all of the pictures on page 194. Follow the directions to glue those pictures on this picture scene.

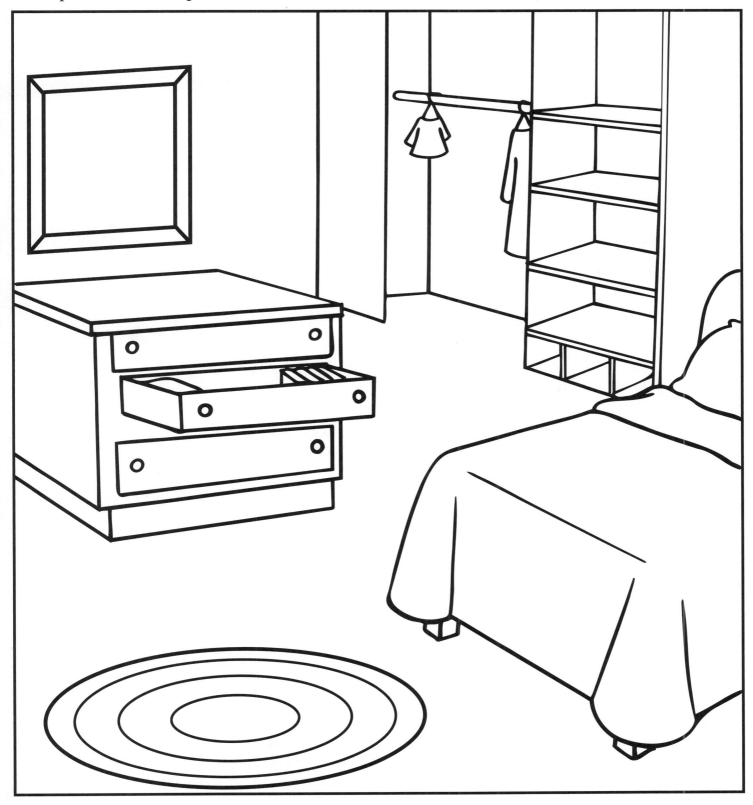

#BK-307 Say & Glue® for Language & Listening Fun Sheets • ©2003 Super Duper® Publications • www.superduperinc.com • 1-800-277-8737

Extention Activities for Categories

Extension activities give the therapist and parent an opportunity to reinforce the target skills at home and school.

1. Play "Hide and Seek." When a person is found, they have to say where they were hiding (e.g., behind the chair).

2. Hide several small objects. When the child finds one, they have to tell where they found it (e.g., under the table).

3. Name an object in the room and have the child tell you where it is (e.g., next to the book).

4. Name places for the child to move and see if they can follow the directions (e.g., go behind the couch).

#BK-307 Say & Glue® for Language & Listening Fun Sheets • ©2003 Super Duper® Publications • www.superduperinc.com • 1-800-277-8737

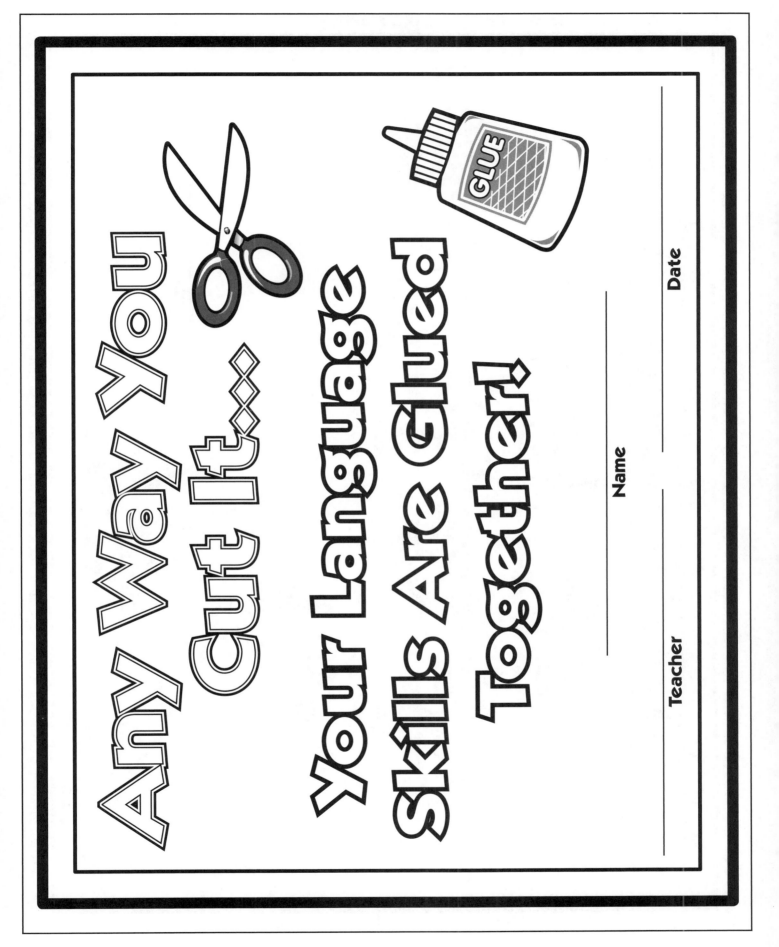

Any Way You Cut It...

Your Language Skills Are Glued Together!

Name

Date

Teacher

Your Listening Skills are Picture Perfect!

Name _____

Teacher _____

Date _____

COOK-OUT!

GLUE

#BK-307 Say & Glue® for Language & Listening Fun Sheets • ©2003 Super Duper® Publications • www.superduperinc.com • 1-800-277-8737